On the God of the Christians
(and on one or two others)

Rémi Brague

Translated by Paul Seaton

St. Augustine's Press
South Bend, Indiana

Originally published as *Du Dieu des chrétiens*
© Flammarion, SA, Paris, France
Translation copyright © 2013 by St. Augustine's Press

Manufactured in the United States of America

1 2 3 4 5 6   19 18 17 16 15 14 13

Library of Congress Cataloging in Publication Data
Brague, Rémi, 1947–
[Du Dieu des chritiens. English]
On the God of the Christians: and on one or two others /
Rémi Brague; translated by Paul Seaton.
p. cm.
Includes index.
ISBN 978-1-58731-345-5 (alk. paper)
1. God (Christianity). 2. Christianity and other religions.
3. Abrahamic religions. I. Seaton, Paul, 1954– II. Title.
BT103.B7313 2013
231 – dc23   2012039720

ST. AUGUSTINE'S PRESS
South Bend, Indiana

Contents

Contents

On the God of the Christians
(and of one or two others)

Translator's Introduction

Rémi Brague (1947–) wears many hats. If he did not wear them, one might wonder if they could be worn by one person. To start with, he is a Frenchman who teaches regularly in Germany. We Americans may not find this especially remarkable, but a fellow French thinker, Pierre Manent, has noted a worrisome decline in Franco-German intellectual exchanges, one that bodes ill not just for the countries involved, but for Europe generally. The polyglot Brague is a grand exception. His dual posts in Paris and Munich, and his familiarity with both countries' classical learning and contemporary scholarship, bring to light the deeper cultural meaning, and ongoing possibilities, of the Franco-German relationship at the heart of Europe. While the majority of his footnote citations in *On the God of Christians* are to French texts and authors, more than forty references to German ones indicate that country's significant presence in his thought.

He is an enormously learned scholar, who is also a controversialist, albeit of a distinctive sort (precisely, a very learned one). His main controversial topics begin with Europe, continue with Christianity and Islam, and conclude with modernity. At least since the fall of the Soviet Union, what is Europe? has been a widely discussed question on the continent, generating heat, some precious light, and ongoing debate. As a good European, Brague has done his duty and tried to lay out defining traits of Europe as a cultural entity. He did this most expansively in *Europe, la voie romaine* (in English: *The Eccentric Culture: A Theory of Western Civilization* (2009)). In his telling, Europe is a doubly indebted culture, with imperial Rome acknowledging its cultural inferiority to Hellenism and classical Christianity affirming against Marcion that it makes no sense apart from its Jewish roots. The prototypical European, one could say, was St. Paul (cf. *Acts of the Apostles* 16: 6–10).

This double affirmation of "eccentric" connectedness laid the foundation for the European cultural edifice, and it provides a context for understanding subsequent European developments, including the complicated character of the enormous endeavor called "modernity."=. Brague has explored the "premodern"– "modern" distinction in a number of books, including *The Wisdom of the World: The Human Experience of the Universe in Western Thought* (2004) and *The Law of God: The Philosophical History of An Idea* (2008).

These are pointed exercises in cultural memory undertaken not just for himself but for his contemporary European readers. Many suffer from what Tocqueville diagnosed as modern democrats' inadequate stance toward the past, not to mention the lingering effects of yesterday's philosophies of progress. Humanly speaking, it is highly desirable (although often difficult) to bring one's past, present, and future into equitable relation. Today's Europeans can better understand themselves by knowing where they came from, what sources and ideas shaped them, as well as the major intellectual choices that directed, and redirected, them. Moreover, given human freedom, the past can help illumine the future. None of this implies that reconsideration is simple or redirection easy. Contemporary events, however, tend to make both urgent.

In coming to grips with the nature of Europe, Christianity necessarily came to the fore, involving Brague in contemporary, as well as historical, debates. The same is true (although to a lesser extent) concerning Islam, since the West has had defining relations with it. The brouhaha over the omission of Christianity from among Europe's spiritual, cultural, and moral sources in a proposed European Constitution, as well as debates about the historical origins and true nature of "secularity" have been among the former, while Europe's Muslim populations have provided the occasion for interventions concerning Islam. As a scholar of medieval thought, versed in all three traditions of Judaism,

Christianity, and Islam, he is able to give present-day controversies much needed historical depth (cf. *The Legend of the Middle Ages: Philosophical Explorations of Medieval Christianity, Judaism, and Islam* (2009), as well as "Secularity versus secularism: an enlightening distinction," www.mercatornet.com, Oct. 7, 2010).

At the highest levels, he can critically engage with Leo Strauss concerning the medieval debates over the truth of the religions (or "divine laws"), as well as the relationship between faith and philosophy. An equal to Strauss in the relevant linguistic and textual learning, and agreeing with Strauss on the fact of esoteric writing, he is able to appreciate Strauss's groundbreaking contributions *and* credibly to charge him with the "Mecca-nization" of Greek philosophy, as well as biblical faith (cf. "Athens, Jerusalem, Mecca: Leo Strauss's 'Muslim' Understanding of Greek Philosophy" (*Poetics Today* 19, no. 2, pp. 235–59)). At more popular levels, he can call to account easy-going democratic hopes concerning "the three religions of the book" or "the three Abrahamic religions" (cf. Chapter 1). Common ground for inter-religious dialogue is not so easily found.

Brague is particularly well-suited to treat these interconnected themes as he is more than a learned scholar, he is a philosopher and a Catholic believer. The motto of the philosopher, "we must distinguish . . . ," comes regularly to his pen. This does not mean he is a terribly abstract thinker, much less that he is a logic-chopper. He can write touchingly of the realities of human love, as well as lay out clearly the Aristotelian senses of "unity" and "relation," bringing both to bear upon his subject. Tellingly, *On the God of Christians* is dedicated to his wife of more than forty years, Françoise, who made "precious suggestions" concerning its content. Here is a conjugal bond consisting in *erôs, agapē*, and *dialogia*. Thus, while illustrating the connections among human persons, freedom, love, knowledge, and mystery, he can write: "It is now forty years that I do *not* know my wife."

Drawing from personal experience as well as from his philosophically informed theological tact, Brague warns throughout the study of the dangers of taking any human experience or reality, be it interpersonal or political, as anything more than a halting "image" of the divine, always to be critically sifted. This, he hastens to add, does not mean that all images are created equal. One must reflect, one must make distinctions. He therefore constantly balances probing investigation into divine matters with an acute sense of the strictures of *theologia negativa*. His feet are very much on the ground, while his gaze surveys the heavens.

And in-between, he is very attuned to the wider human world. His ears and critical intelligence are attentive to the twin discourses of academe and the democratic city. The treasure trove of citations found at the bottom of the text can set the interested reader off on any number of intellectual adventures. Similarly, I invite the reader to pay particular attention to the picture of contemporary democracy limned in these pages, as well as to a figure he calls "modern man." Implicit in them, by way of contrast, is a portrait of the thoughtful believer in the contemporary city. Brague would be too modest to call it a self-portrait, so I will do so.

In these ways, Brague reminds me of a number of other thinkers. I will mention one. His intellectual *erôs* combined with candid recognition of mysteries, his bold taking-on and equitable taking-the-measure of controverted topics, his dialectical approach, and his delight in paradox and in opening new horizons – all this reminds me of Socrates. I am tempted to call Brague a Catholic Socratic, because of his intrepid making of distinctions even when they might be unwelcome, together with his theological "knowledge of ignorance" that combines, in exquisite proportions, experience and learning, belief and reasoning, mystery and discernment. I would also give him the moniker because in this study rather bold exegetical and philosophical reflection precedent over simple dogmatic affirmation. His treatment of the biblical images of "the vineyard" and "the vine" common to both testaments is a case in point, as are his reflections upon divine and human "naming" at the beginning of the Bible (Chapter 6).

To be sure, Brague is unmistakably a Catholic Christian, and his theme is the God confessed by Christians. That God is One and Triune, Father, Eternal Logos and Incarnate Son, and Holy Spirit. All these "attributes" (and more) are surveyed by him, assisted by accredited theological guides such as St. Bernard of Clairvaux (Chapter 3) and St. John of the Cross (Chapter 5). Still, the philosopher's perspective and learning are always present. They dictate his insistence upon linking biblical narrative with the Greek philosophical notion of *phusis*, a connection he develops in several directions. It is here that he enters, I believe, into the thorniest theoretical matters with which he deals. To list them is to indicate their importance: the relationship between the concepts of creation and nature, of providence, freedom, and history, of the good, both natural and supernatural, and, finally, of sin and forgiveness. All these are treated in terms of God's providential care for created natures, especially his human creature, for whom the divinely intended good is filiation and friendship with his fatherly Creator. Admittedly, the "incomplete" treatment of his subject entails that he must raise these topics and that he cannot adequately treat them. Nonetheless, for both Brague and the active reader, the *logos* beckons, if not compels.

Be that as it may, the interpenetration of philosophy and faith in Brague's thought is also evident in his insistence upon the *personal* character of human being. To speak of human nature is both necessary and insufficient in Brague's view. Freedom finally precedent over nature in man, but in ways indicated by biblical affirmations, not Kantian autonomy or contemporary notions of self-creation. The Christian God has distinctive ideas about his privileged creature, the one made in his image and likeness. What is often called "Christian personalism" tries to comprehend them. In so doing, it gratefully receives philosophy's assistance as well as challenges its offerings and its adequacy. Here, in this ambiguous endeavor, one especially observes an acrobat of the spirit in action.

In general, to read the *oeuvre* of Rémi Brague is to receive an expertly guided tour of western civilization, focused through the prism of such important topics as cosmos and wisdom, "law" divine, natural, and human, as well as nature, freedom, and grace, all framed by the overarching categories of premodern and modern, all comprehended as core elements of Western culture. In previous books, the Catholic philosopher undertook the great adventure of seeking self-knowledge, with the identities of "Western" and "European" marking his way. He did so, though, by somewhat indirect means, via what might appear to be "merely" cultural or historical investigations. *On the God of Christians* continues the path of exploration begun by Brague several decades ago. Now, though, he makes its personal character rather clear. His is a mind and heart characterized by *fides quaerens intellectum*. In a way that at times brings to mind Augustine's *Confessions*, he now displays this animating motive for all to see, to consider, and, perhaps, to take to heart.

Paul Seaton
St. Mary's Seminary & University
Feast of the Epiphany, 2012

Author's Foreword

Let us begin with two grand truisms: In himself, God is the same for all. Secondly, he is beyond all the representations that men have made of him.

Having knocked open these open doors, let us move on to serious things. What is truly interesting is that the images and concepts that have been made of God (which concepts are themselves, at bottom, but images) differ among men and among the associations that bring men together, whether it be philosophical schools or religions. Therefore, if we cannot directly grasp what (or better: who) God is in and for himself, this inability leads us back to the existing diversity of representations of him, and lays upon us the task of getting clear about the nuances, or chasms, that divide them.

The goal of this book is in no way to provide anything approaching a "theory of God." It has no other aim than to describe the image made of him by a certain religion (Christianity), while not ruling out comparisons with the images made of him by other past, or current, religions. I therefore treat the God of Christians, not, as is sometimes said, "the Christian God." That is an absurd formulation, since God is the object of the religions, not one of their adherents. God alone has the right to be an atheist.

I hope to have written a book of philosophy, or at least a book by someone who would like to be a philosopher. Not, however, without casting a respectful eye on theology, considered as a discipline that is at least as self-consciously critical as my own. Theology in fact is the sole discipline that begins by interrogating itself about what the other forms of knowledge assume, to wit: the very existence of the object it studies. And it does not advance, except by constantly seeking an even purer meaning of the substantive "God" and the verb "to exist."

I do not have the intention of making God's existence more plausible by adducing "proofs" (a term that the best theologians avoid, or only employ with a thousand caveats). I simply want to show that a certain image of God, the one that Christianity adduces, possesses traits that distinguish it from certain other images. In order to do so, I first of all will dispose of certain widespread confusions, which are necessary to avoid if one does not want to get off on the wrong foot (Chapter 1). I then will address what it can mean "to know God" (Chapter 2). Then I will examine certain features of God: He is one, but not in just any manner (Chapter 3); He is Father, but not male (Chapter 4); He spoke, but not to ask anything of us (Chapter 5); He forgives, but not by ignoring the exercise of our freedom (Chapter 6).

The image that I provide of Christianity is, therefore, obviously incomplete. I neither wanted, nor could have, spoken about everything. Likewise, I am far from considering it to be perfect. The reader is welcome to improve or correct it. *A fortiori*, I do not claim to have presented an exhaustive image of God that the other religions that are treated here present. These are only invoked in a comparison intended to highlight the singularity of Christianity. The somewhat flippant title and subtitle of the present work thus serve to underscore the incomplete character of the inquiry.

As for the God that Christianity images, whether well or not, the reader can accept or reject him. No one needs my permission. I only hope that in either case, it will be done with a bit more knowledge of the case.

Françoise, my wife, agreed to reread my manuscript and gave me precious suggestions. I hope she will permit me to dedicate this book to her on the fortieth anniversary of our first meeting. I have equally benefited from the pertinent observations of Irene Fernandez, whom I cordially thank.

R. B.
Paris, December 2007

Chapter 1
Disposing of Three Trios

The past several years, three expressions have entered the medias when it comes to talking about religion. Each time, it is a question of three things: "the three monotheisms," "the three religions of Abraham," "the three religions of the book." It is difficult to come across an organ of the press or to pick up a paper (be it religious or secular) without having one or another of these formulations put forth as self-evident. At a higher level, books that have one of them as titles, or which contain them (some of which are of high quality) have multiplied since the 1980s.[1]

It would be interesting to study the history of these expressions – something I have not had the courage to do. I would be tempted to venture, in lieu of an inventory, that the genealogy of these expressions could very well go back to the Middle Ages; and more exactly, that the idea of associating Judaism, Christianity, and Islam come from a desire to condemn them all rather than embracing them in a common sympathy! In this way, what are called today "the three religions" would simply be the latest version of what was applied long ago to "the three impostors," Moses, Jesus, and Mohammed, deemed to have deceived humanity.

---

1 The first book that bore the express title *Les Trois Monothéismes* was a work by the psychoanalyst D. Sibony, which had as its subtitle *Juifs, Chrétiens et Musulmans entre leurs sources et leurs destins* (Paris, Le Seuil, 1992). The philosopher and scholar of Islam R. Arnaldez published *Trois messagers pour un seul Dieu* (Paris, Albin Michel, 1983), and *À la croisée des trois monothéismes. Une communauté de pensée au Moyen Age* (Paris, Albin Michel, 1993).

In any event, one can believe that these expressions were more recently conceived, and continue to be used, out of noble motives. These would indicate a point in common for the religions in question, eventually some common ground in practice.

My immediate purpose is to show that these three expressions are at once false and dangerous. They are *false* because each masks a serious error concerning the nature of the three religions that one claims to bring together under a common roof. They are *dangerous* because they encourage an intellectual sloth that relieves one of closely examining reality. I will examine them in order, starting with the idea of "monotheism."

I. Three monotheisms?

The term "monotheism" comes from outside, not within, religions. The "monotheisms" do not speak of themselves this way. To be sure, certain expressions they use allow themselves to be translated in this way, such as the Arab *tawhîd*, "affirmation that God is one" – a word that, by extension, took on a meaning close to "theology." Speaking very precisely, among some Jews there is a characterization of Judaism as "ethical monotheism," a phrase that, perhaps, is attributable to the German rabbi Leo Baeck (1873–1956).

The term "monotheism" was born rather late, in the seventeenth century, from the pen of Henry More, one of the Christian Platonists of Cambridge, who used it in English in 1660 (see the *Oxford English Dictionary*, "monotheism"). Its subsequent career saw it occur much more among the philosophers than the theologians, and almost never was it used as an expression of piety by simple believers.

1. Monotheism is not essentially religious.
Let us begin with a synthetic statement: monotheism – and, moreover, polytheism – has nothing specifically religious in its meaning; it primarily comes from philosophy.

There are non-monotheistic religions that exist. But, conversely, there are non-religious monotheisms, in which one finds a philosophical affirmation of a God who is not the object of a religion. This is the case with the deism of certain Enlightenment thinkers. Here, though, we can always ask if this does not involve a certain weakened version of Christianity, in which only an answer to the question of the number of gods was retained. The best examples, therefore, should be sought among the Greek philosophers who never heard of Judaism and, even less, of Christianity. Thus, the presocratic Xenophanes of Colophon (who lived in the 6th–5th century before Christ) opposed to the various imaginings of the nations, each of whom represented the deity in their image, "a sole god, the greatest among the gods and men, who resembles mortals neither in appearance nor in thought."[2] After him, Aristotle called the unchanging first mover of his natural philosophy by the name of "god." It appears that this god knows nothing outside of itself.[3]

In contrast, Epicurus admitted the existence of several gods. They live in the interstices separating the innumerable worlds postulated by his cosmology. They enjoyed a perfect beatitude and took no thought, and had no concern, for those worlds and their inhabitants.[4] The philosopher publicly acknowledged the gods of the city and rendered them appropriate worship, but did not consider them to be true gods.

The affirmation of a sole God is therefore not necessarily a religious phenomenon. One can have a God without religion. Conversely, one can have a religion without God, as was the case with primitive Buddhism.

2   Xenophanes, Diels and Kranz, fragment 21 B 23.
3   Aristotle, *Metaphysics*, 12, 7, 1072b25, 29–30.
4   See my work, *La Sagesse du monde. Histoire de l'expérience humaine de l'univers* (Paris, Fayard, 1999), pp. 54–55 (English: *Wisdom of the World: the Human Experience f the Universe in Western Thought* [Chicago: University of Chicago Press, 2004], pp. 40–41).

2. There are not only three monotheisms.

When one says "the three monotheisms," the use of the definite article assumes that there are only three. However, these purported "three monotheisms" were not the first. The first was, perhaps, the invention of the Pharaoh Amenophis IV, who took the name Akhnaton (1250 B.C.E.). The underlying idea is that a sole God is the true one, the others only being subordinate delegates. In its case, Israel began with a national God, to whom alone worship should be given, but the other gods were the legitimate gods of the neighboring nations. It was only after the return from exile that the idea emerged that there is but one God, the other gods being false, that is, "idols" (*Isaiah* 44, 8; 47, 21).

These "three monotheisms" were also not the last. Religious fecundity did not dry up, especially among the colonized peoples of the Third World (Voodoo and Pentacostalism among African blacks) or who had had contact with the West (the Cargo cult in New Guinea). In contrast, almost no one invented new poly-theisms. Religions emerge most often from a preexisting religion that they claim to reform. And these "maternal" religions are monotheistic. Thus, in the nineteen century religions such as Mormonism were born from Christianity and the Bahai religion from Islam. The religion of the Sikhs, born in the seventeenth century from Hinduism, borrowed monotheism from Islam.

The new religions of today understand themselves as adjuncts to preexisting religions, for example, Kimbanguism, born in the 1930s in the Republic of Congo (then the Belgian Congo) from the preaching of Simon Kimbangu, which succeeded in being admitted into the ecumenical Council of Churches. This is rare, since the older religions most often find it hard to admit that the new religions can claim to represent a legitimate version of themselves. Thus, Judaism does not accept Christianity, Christianity does not accept Islam, and the latter in turn does not accept Bahaism.

3. Do monotheism and polytheism simply oppose one another?

The real question is not the quantity of gods. It is never a matter of merely determining their number by counting. In fact, one can wonder if a veritable polytheism has ever existed outside of the polemics of those who attack it. Aristotle distinguishes different sorts of unity or, more concretely, different cases when one says "it is the same thing." He therefore distinguishes unity by number (the same thing, which "does not constitute number"), by species (you and I are members of the human race), by genus (my dog and I are living beings), and by analogy (scales and feathers are the same thing, because scales are to fish what feathers are to birds).[5] One can say that every religion attributes to the divine one or another of these different levels of unity. The divine can present itself as an individual, a family, a teeming race, a level of being. In each case, though, it is distinguished from what it is not, i.e., the "profane," by characteristics that constitute it as a unity. As a consequence, the proper question is to ask what the monotheism makes of plurality, and what the polytheism makes of unity.[6]

Ancient paganism knew the idea of a "world" of the divine, a pantheon that made all the gods members of a single, and unique, collectivity. This is what Homer said so magnificently: "The gods are not unknown to one another, even if they live in separate dwellings" (*Odyssey*, V, 79–80). And above the family of the Olympians hovered Destiny (*Moira*), which regulated the succession of the generations constituting the family. Fathers were dethroned in favor of their sons. Perhaps it was this impersonal power that, for the Greeks, was the veritable cause of the unity of the divine.

4. The real question

The real question, therefore, is to ask *how* God is one, what is the mode of unity that relates the divine to itself. Here I will simply sketch a point that I will develop later (Chapter 3). "To be one": that can mean to affirm that God is unique. There is only one. The set "gods" only contains one member. Here, however, one encounters a

---

5 Aristotle, *Metaphysics*, V, 6, 1016, b31–35.

6 This is the question P. Gisel poses in his work, *Les Monothéismes. Judaïsme, christianisme, islam, 145 Propositions* (Geneva, Labor et Fides, 2006), p. 13.

paradox that arises from rather simple logic. Unity, like every number, is not the property of the thing, but of the class to which it belongs. To say that God is one, is to suppose that he belongs to a higher class, that of "unities." Thus, while one thinks that by affirming God's unity one is making him something supreme, in reality one is devaluing him, because he is subordinated to the class of unities.

This is why religions do not content themselves with affirming that God only exists as a single exemplar (his "uniqueness"). They also say something about the way in which he is one with himself (his "unity").

God can be one by way of continuity with himself, because he is, as it were, of a single piece. The Quran offers a representation of this sort when, in a famous sura which was often invoked against the Christian idea of the Trinity, it calls God "the Impenetrable" (as-samad) (112, 2). Even the most ancient commentators did not understand the meaning of the adjective, and they had to venture conjectures. They sometimes explained that God is wholly continuous or homogenous, without imperfection, without defect, like a piece of forged metal.[7]

God can be one by way of fidelity to himself in the context of a design of salvation being worked out in history. This, perhaps, is what is expressed by the famous formula in the Book of Exodus by which the God of Israel presented himself to Moses, calling himself "I will be He whom I will be." (*Exodus* 3, 14).

God can be one by way of the total accord, in love, of the three hypostases of the divine substance. For Christianity, the Trinity is *not* a way of attenuating the rigor of monotheism. To the contrary, it is a way of thinking to a conclusion *how* God is one. If "God is love" (1 *John* 4, 16), it is love that must constitute the internal law of his being, and thus of his unity with himself. (As I said, I will develop these thoughts later in the work.)

I do not like it therefore when, as often happens, it is said (whether to credit or discredit them makes no difference) that

---

7   D. Gimaret, *Les Noms divins en Islam. Exégèse lexico-graphique et théologique* (Paris, Le Cerf, 1988), pp. 320–23.

Islam or Judaism profess a "strict monotheism." This is as though there could be "less strict" monotheisms, Christianity, for example. It is enough simply to try to imagine what a relaxed monotheism – one that is accommodating, easy-going – to see the absurdity of this sort of formulation. God is not *more or less* one. . . . The difference is not in the harder or softer character of the monotheism, but in the way in which the unity is conceived.

5. *Islamic monotheism*

It was not Islam that discovered the unique God, "The-God," Allah. He was already known to the Arabs. "If you ask them: 'Who created heaven and earth, who subjected the sun and the moon?', they answer: "God!" . . . ."[8] The Allah before Mohammed was, perhaps, what the historians of religion call an "idle god" (*deus otiosus*). Such a God creates the world, then retires, letting lesser divinities administer the created order and share the prayers and sacrifices of men. Islam, therefore, would be a sort of short-circuit, passing by the divinities tasked with interceding, in order to arrive directly at the creator God.

We however are not very clear about the religion of the Arabs at the time of Mohammed. The traditional history supposes that they, in the main, were pagans, polytheists therefore, with a few Christian tribes, some Jewish ones, and a small number of isolated individuals given the mysterious name of *hanîf*, we could say: monotheists without any particular denomination. Arab historians have collected the data pertaining to the idols worshipped in ancient Araby.[9] It seems, however, that they attributed to the epoch of Mohammed a religious situation that had already disappeared for several centuries, and that the Araby of the time was much more Christianized than was generally thought. The Quran speaks often

---

8   Quran, XXIX, 61, XXXI, 25, XXXIX, 38; cf. XLIII, 9 ("the Powerful, the Knowing"); ". . . who created them . . ." (XLIII, 87).

9   See, for instance, Hicham Ibn al-Kalbî, *Les Idoles* [Kitâb al-Asnâm], a text established and translated by W. Atallah (Paris, Klincksieck, 1969).

of the "associators" (*mushrikûn*), those who associate one, or several other beings, with the unique God. And it does so in rather harsh terms. Who were they, though? Pagans? Or rather Christians, adherents of Trinitarian doctrine as it had been interpreted by those who rejected the dogma defined at the Council of Nicea concerning Christ, that he is "of one substance with the Father"? Some have thought so, with arguments that do not lack in value.[10]

6. A mutual recognition of the monotheisms?

It is at least paradoxical to see monotheism as an element common to the three religions, since it historically functioned as a golden apple, that is, an apple of discord. In fact, these three religions only recognize the others as monotheistic with great difficulty.

Christianity does recognize the monotheism of Judaism. Judaism finds it harder to return the favor. Employing a phrase from the Quran (V, 73), Maimonides reproached Christians with making God "the third of three."[11] It was not until the Rabbi of Perpignan Menahem ha-Meiri (d. 1315) that the dominant opinion (although not unanimous) became that Christians are not "idolators."[12]

Judaism recognized the monotheism of Muslims, once the misunderstanding was cleared up concerning the worship offered to the Kaaba.[13] Islam would without difficulty recognize the

---

10 See G. R. Hawting, *The Idea of Idolatry and the Emergence of Islam: From Polemic to History* (Cambridge University Press, 1999); and E. M. Gallez, *Le Messie et son prophète. Aux origins de l'Islam* (Versailles, Editions de Paris, 2005).

11 Maimonides, *Tractate on Resurrection*, #1, in *Iggerot. Letters*, ed. J. Kafih (Jerusalem, Mosad ha-Rav Kook), p. 69 [Transl. H. Fradkin in R. Lerner, *Maimonides' Empire of Light. Popular Enlightenment in an Age of Belief*, Chicago: The University of Chicago Press, 2000, p. 154].

12 Menahem ha-Meiri, *Beth ha-Behira*, on 'Avoda Zara, 53 [*non vidi*].

13 Maimonides, *Lettre sur la persécution*, chap. 2, in *Iggerot. Letters*, *op. cit.*, p. 112 ; "Answer to Ovadia the Proselyte," in *Responsa*, ed. J. Blau (Jerusalem, Mass, 1989), t. 2, p. 726.

monotheism of Jews, if the Quran did not reproach them for associating a mysterious personage named 'Uzayr (IX, 30) with God.
Perhaps this is the Esdras of the Bible, unless it is the garbled name
of an angel.

Christianity today considers the monotheistic character of Islam
to be obvious. It was not always thus, however. John of Damascus,
one of the first Christians to write on the religion of the "Ismaelites,"
turns the charge that Christians adore the Cross to the counter-
charge of worshiping the Black Rock of Kaaba. And the popular literature of the Middle Ages saw Muslims as pagans, adoring
Mohammed and two other idols![14] For their part, many Muslims
admit that Christians are not polytheists. But what to make of the
formulas in the Quran which formally accuse them of associating
"monks," or even Jesus and his Mother, with God (IX, 31; V, 116)?

Thus, to speak of the religions as "monotheistic" does not get
us very far in understanding them. One still has to ask, what
model of divine unity is at work, and what are the consequences
of the application of the model? In other words, what is the meaning of this-or-that affirmation of divine unity?

II. Three religions of Abraham?

By the phrases "the three religions of Abraham" or "the three
Abrahamic religions," people believe they establish common
ground, by appealing to a common ancestor. In truth, however,
this is another golden apple.

1. *The common personages*
All three, Judaism, Christianity, and Islam, have books in which
the name of a person named Abraham appears. (The Arabic of the

---

14 J. Damascene, *Hérésie* 100, #5, in *Écrits sur l'Islam*, ed. R. Le Coz
(Paris, Le Cerf (*Sources chrétiennes*, n. 383), pp. 218–20; *La
Chanson de Roland*, I, v. 8, ed. T. A. Jenkins (Boston, Heath, 1924),
p. 4; XXXII, vv. 416–17, p. 40; XLVII, v. 611, p. 53; etc.

Quran writes with a slight variation: Ibrahîm. This, perhaps, is due to a later incorrect reading of an obsolete form of writing.[15]) Abraham, however, is not the only biblical personage whose name is common to all the religions. This is also the case for Adam, Noah, Joseph, Moses, and Jonah, who appear in the Old and New Testaments as well as the Quran. In its turn, the Quran knows Jesus and his mother, the Virgin Mary, while the foundational writings of Judaism obviously do not mention them.

Islam, though, gives to the one that Christians name Jesus a very different name than the one by which he was known to the Jews (Yeshu), as well as by Christian Arabs (Yasû'). The Quran calls him 'Issâ, a name that recalls in a surprising way that of Esaü ('Issaw). In this, should one see the trace of an implicit comparison of the three religions? That of the Jews coming from Jacob (Israël), the Arabs from Ismaël, and Christians from Esaü? It is well known that Jewish texts often identified Christians in a symbolic way with Esaü.

At a more general level a problem arises, that of the presence in the three religions of literary figures bearing the same name. Simply because the names are the same does not mean that the personages are. Their personal traits are embedded and revealed in the particular narratives of the different writings. And what is recounted in the holy books of the three religions with respect to these figures is not uniform, far from it. The history of Joseph is the only one that the Quran recounts in an integral, orderly way, in sura XII, entitled "Joseph" (*Yûsuf*). It reprises the grand features of the biblical account (*Genesis*, 37–50), and adds some details drawn from the Jewish legends found in the Midrash.[16] The same thing can be said, *grosso modo*, of the figure of Moses.

15 See C. Luxenberg, *Die syro-aramäische Lesart des Koran. Ein Beitrag zur Entschlüsselung der Koransprache*, s. l., (Schiler, 2004 [2nd ed.]), pp. 102–3 (English: *The Syro-Aramaic Reading of the Koran: A Contribution to the Decoding of the Language of the Koran* [Verlag Hans Schiler, 2007]).

16 See A.–L. de Prémare, *Joseph et Muhammad. Le chapitre 12 du Coran*, (Aix-en-Provence, Université de Provence, 1989).

Moreover, the meaning of the biblical figures does not solely depend upon these individual narratives looked at in isolation. It also depends in large part upon the connections among them which shed reciprocal light. The meaning of the figure of Mary in Christianity is hardly conceivable without the "typological" connection between her and Eve, which is not found in Islam.[17]

But it is with respect to Jesus that the Quran and the New Testament differ the most. The miracles reported in the Quran are healings, which are not specified. The Quran adds spectacular miracles, in which the embellishing of the apocryphal Gospels makes itself seen: Jesus speaking as an infant, or creating birds of bronze, animating them, then destroying them (III, 49; V, 110). Jesus's teaching is not reported. Finally, Jesus was not crucified by the Jews, it only "seemed to them" (*shubbiha lahum*) that he had been (IV, 157). Taken up to heaven, he had not died and therefore did not need to be resurrected.

2. The same Abraham?

As for the figure of Abraham, it is rather a source of disagreement than of concord. In truth, for Judaism and for Christianity, Islam is not Abrahamic. It is not in its conception of prophecy, nor in its conception of history. Jesus, the Twelve, Paul and the first Christians, were all Jews. They thus linked themselves to an Abrahamic genealogy that no one contested. The problem only surfaced when Paul had believers of Gentile origin admitted into the Christian community. He justified this enlargement by interpreting the story of the two sons of Abraham, the son of the slave Hagar and the son of Sarah, the free woman, with the first representing "the flesh," the second "the spirit" (*Galatians* 4, 21–31).

Mohammed and the first Muslims were not of Jewish stock and did not live in the Holy Land. They, therefore, had to attach themselves to the biblical history by inventing a genealogy. They constructed one by also representing the history of two of Abraham's sons. In the Bible, Ishmaël was the ancestor of the

17 See P. Gisel, *Les Monothéismes, op. cit.*, p. 134.

desert nomads (*Genesis* 16, 12). One only had to see in them the Arabs for the equation to be made. It does not appear that the idea of connecting themselves to Ishmaël came to the Arabs before Mohammed. No previous genealogy of biblical inspiration existed before the Islamic enterprise.[18]

The history of Abraham is not interpreted in the same way in Judaism and in Christianity. Both underscore the extraordinary faith of the patriarch, who was ready to sacrifice the son that God had promised him. Judaism prefers to put the accent upon the non-sacrifice of Isaac. In fact, it does not talk about the *sacrifice* of the son, but his "binding" (*'aqèdah*), with the child having been bound, as one did with the animals of the Temple. The central event is God's intervention, as He restrains the hand of Abraham and substitutes a ram for the human victim. Christianity adds to the example of Abraham's faith an allegorical reading of his sacrifice as a prefiguration of the cross of Christ. Everything is turned upside down: it is God himself who sacrifices his beloved Son. The situation of Islam is more complex. The Quran leaves vague the identity of the son who was to be sacrificed. Was it to have been Isaac, as in the Bible? Or Ishmaël?

Moreover, the Quran places Abraham in a series of prophets who would have received a book, projecting backwards the model of Mohammed. Abraham is therefore deemed to have received, like Moses, pages or "leaves" (Quran, LIII, 37; LXXXVII, 19; see XX, 133), which neither the Old nor the New Testament mentions. Above all, the Quran makes use of the figure of Abraham to recount a history that neither Judaism nor Christianity knows anything about, and for good reason: that of the foundation of a house by the patriarch (Quran, II, 125–127). The word (*bayt*) can mean "temple," and the purpose of the edifice clearly shows that this is the case: one had to bow and prostrate oneself therein (Quran, XXII, 26). The Quran does not say anything about the particular location of this building, but the subsequent Islamic

18 See R. Dagorn, *La Geste d'Ismaël d'après l'onomastique et la tradition arabes* (Geneva, Droz, 1981).

tradition placed it in the "sterile valley," that of Mecca, and saw in the house, the cubic temple of the Kaaba. This furnished the pilgrimage to them with a legitimacy that went back to the oldest antiquity.

3. Three religions of Abraham, or only one?

In the West, one has the habit of speaking of the "religions of Abraham" in the plural. This, above all, is a Christian locution. For Islam there is *only one* "religion of Abraham," which is Islam itself. For the Christian, to speak of the "religion of Abraham" is to include Judaism and Islam, and to associate them with Christianity in a vague sort of fraternity. For Islam, on the other hand, it means to exclude Judaism and Christianity: "Abraham was neither a Jew nor a Christian, but a true believer (*hanîf*) and Muslim (*muslim*), and he was not one of the polytheists (*mushrik*)" (Quran, III, 67).[19] This exclusion operates by a series of retrenchments. The operation is already found in the Quran: "They have said: 'Be Jews or Christians, you will be well advised.'" Say: "But no! . . . Follow the religion of Abraham, a true believer who was not numbered among the polytheists" (II, 135). For the Muslim religion, Islam already was the religion of Abraham. This religion of Abraham, anterior to Judaism as well as Christianity, was moreover already that of Moses, Noah, and even Adam, as it was later the religion of Jesus. It was the religion of all of the humanity which was to come from the loins of Adam. This was a humanity which even before the creation of the world, miraculously drawn from its first ancestor, confessed the lordship of God, in a scene described in the Quran (VII, 172).

What, then, is the status of the two other religions, apparently chronologically anterior to the religion preached by Mohammed? The main current of Islam sees in them deformations, betrayals of the message originally addressed to Abraham.

---

19 I give these three key terms the meaning that they have in traditional Muslim exegesis. These words are obscure and their interpretation, especially the word *muslim*, anachronistic.

This derives logically from the fundamental teaching of the deformation (*tahrîf*) of the previous Scriptures.[20] It is derived from the interpretation of the verses of the Quran: "certain Jews altered [the meaning] of the [revealed] words" (IV, 46 and V, 13; V, 41; II, 75). The meaning of these Quranic verses is not totally clear, but the passages most often were interpreted as signifying that the sacred texts were tampered with. The common view is the following: the Jews imagine that they have in their hands the Torah revealed to Moses, the Christians believe they possess "the Gospel" (in the singular) which was revealed to the prophet Jesus. But the two books, the Torah and the Gospel, were corrupted, the first by the Jews, the second by the Christians, which deprives both of the genuineness they claim. Those guilty for these deformations are sometimes identified: Esdras for the Torah, St. Paul for the Gospel. Happily, the authentic content of the revelations made to Moses and to Jesus was preserved, precisely in the Quran.

Thanks to its invocation of Abraham, Islam effects a paradoxical operation according to which, on one hand, it is the last of the religions, on the other, the first of all of them.

Thus, the "Abraham" that the three religions would have in common is a vague abstraction. This smallest of common denominators coincides with none of the concrete figures revered by them and in which they recognize themselves. To accept such an Abraham would be for each religion to renounce a dimension of its faith.

20 See my work, *La Loi de Dieu. Histoire philosophique d'une alliance* (Paris, Gallimard, 2005), pp. 117–19 (English: *The Law of God: The Philosophical History of an Idea* [Chicago, University of Chicago Press, 2001, 2008]) and above all, H. Lazarus-Yafeh, *Intertwined Worlds. Medieval Islam and Bible Criticism* (Princeton, Princeton University Press, 1992). The Indian reformer Ahmad Khan (1817–1898) – against whom Jamâl ed-Dîn el-Afghanî wrote the *Refutation of Materialists* – seems to have been the first to propose the abandonment of this teaching. See P. Gisel, *The Monotheisms*, *op. cit.*, p.124.

III. Three religions of the book?

1. *A deceptive expression*

Among Christians and Jews, but also among certain Muslims, one speaks of "three religions of the book." The expression is deceptive. First of all, because it already has a meaning in one of the religions, Islam. Islamic law has the concept of "people of the book" (*ahl al-kitâb*). In the Islamic city, there is no place for pagans, who, in principle, have the choice between conversion and death only. In contrast, the members of the religions that already had a sacred text when Mohammed came on the scene, i.e., Judaism and Christianity, as well as Zoroastrianism, do have a juridically defined place by rules that fix the rights and duties of the "protected" communities (*ahl al-dhimma*). Islam, however, clearly does not consider itself as being a part of these "peoples of the book."

The second defect of this expression is its imprecision. Does a "religion of the book" signify a religion in which there is found a sacred book or books? In this sense, every religion coming from a people that knows writing has one or several written texts. These can be narratives, what are called myths, legends concerning the god or the gods of this religion. They can equally be instruments of worship, for example, collections of hymns, of religious songs. They can also be cultic "recipes," as it were, concerning the art and manner of sacrifice, of how to offer gifts to the divinity. One can find in them rules of conduct, of morality, counsels concerning how to please the divinity. Finally, one can find collections of the teachings of the founder of the religion.

It is fitting, therefore, not to identify the religions of a book with the three religions of Judaism, Christianity, and Islam. Moreover, a religion in which there is a book is not, by that fact, a "religion *of the book*." And finally, even if one limits oneself to Judaism, Christianity, and Islam, one has to make distinctions because, as we will see, the relation of each of these religions to its own book is not the same in each case.

2. Three very different books

This is explained, first of all, by the difference in the nature of these three books. They were redacted according to different rhythms, accelerating as one progressed. The period of redaction for the Old Testament was approximately eight centuries, for the New Testament about seventy years, for the Quran, about twenty years. Moreover, they were not composed with the same aim in mind. The texts brought together in the Old and New Testaments, composed by different authors, in different contexts and for different reasons, only formed a sacred book once they were assembled and deemed canonical. In contrast, the Quran seems to have been composed in order to serve as the sacred book of a community. It situates itself in this way in a series of works that probably began in the third century C.E., with the book of Mani, the founder of Manicheanism, and which continued as late as the nineteenth century with the book of the Bahais, the Book of Mormon, and many others.[21]

a) The Old Testament

The Old Testament is less a book than a library, a collection of books that belong to all the literary genres. There you find history, whether actual or mythic, legislation, poetry, including erotic poetry such as the *Song of Songs*, quasi-philosophic writing, e.g., *Ecclesiastes*, prophetic exhortations, and the so-called "Wisdom" literature. Its oldest texts probably date back to 1200 B.C.E., while the most recent differ somewhat between Jews and Christians. The Jews only accept the texts written in Hebrew and in Aramaic, while Christians add texts translated into Greek (*Sirach*) or written directly in that language (*Wisdom*), which include some that emerged in the first century before Christ.

During the course of these thousands of years of redaction, later texts contained reflections upon the previous texts, commenting on them, pointing back to them. The fifth book of the

---

21 See the excellent little book of A. Jeffery, *The Qur'ân as Scripture* (New York, Russell F. Moore, 1952).

first five books of the Bible, which Christians call *Deuteronomy* (in Greek: "the second law") and the Jews call "the repetition of the Torah" (*Mishneh Torah*), is a reflection upon the laws contained in the three previous books.

The danger for the reader of the Old Testament is to place all these texts on the same plane, to consider them as if they had the same status, while one must pay the closest attention to the literary genre of each book: historical narrative, poem, parables. . . .

b) The New Testament

The New Testament also contains different literary genres: the four Gospels, the narratives of the life, teachings, and passion of Jesus; the *Acts of the Apostles*, the history of the beginnings of the spread of Christianity; the *Epistles*, letters written by the principal apostles to the communities for which they felt responsible; finally, the *Apocalypse*, a book of revelations. Their authors differ, one can even discern different schools of interpretation of the life of Jesus. Nonetheless, the New Testament presents a greater unity than the Old, it is written in one language, a popular Greek (*koiné*), and its redaction occurred over a few decades only.

c) The Quran

The Quran, at least on the surface, has a greater unity: it is the work of one hand, in which intertexuality abounds (repetitions, citations, allusions). The main difficulty in reading it resides in its very obscure vocabulary, for the very simple reason that the Quran itself is the oldest work in the Arab language that we possess, with the exception of a few inscriptions and, perhaps, certain poems (the so-called "anteislamic poetry") which could have been rewritten at a later date, and adapted to a more recent state of the language for better understanding.[22] We therefore lack a context, a base-line, which allows us to interpret it.

22 This is the hypothesis of the Egyptian Taha Husayn, in a work written in 1926 which rendered him quite suspect, *Fî 'sh-shi'r al-jâhilî* [*Sur la poèsie antéislamique*] (reed. Le Caire, Dâr al-Nahâr, 1995) [*non vidi*].

3. Three relations to the book

With Judaism, Christianity, and Islam we have three religions, each of which has its book, but which has a different relationship with the book. At the risk of oversimplifying, I would express these relations in three formulas that I will develop shortly. The religion of Israel is a history that led to a book; Christianity is a history recounted in a book; Islam is a book that led to a history.

a) Judaism

Let us begin chronologically with Judaism, taken in a large sense. The religion of ancient Israel did not rest exclusively on the existence of a book. It was during the course of its history that the library that we call the Old Testament was composed, and it was composed in circumstances closely connected with the political development of the people.

The religion of ancient Israel is a national religion, a worship offered to its god by a people, in the same way that neighboring peoples offered their worship, hymns, and sacrifices to their gods. This religion had sacrifices, feasts, and places of worship which, at a certain period, were reduced to one: the Temple at Jerusalem, the clergy of which exercised a sort of monopoly.

In the course of this history, a certain number of documents were produced, such as chronicles of kings. A people loves to sing of its glorious ancestors, the patriarchs; this, in part, is the subject of *Genesis*. Israel also codified the civil and penal code the king imposed on his people. Priests wrote down the ritual of the Temple at Jerusalem, as well as its collection of hymns.

Judaism properly speaking, Judaism in the narrow sense, was constituted by a series of tragic events in the history of Israel. Around 70 C.E., to be a Jew could not longer mean being the subject of the king of Israel, nor inhabiting the land since the majority of the Jewish people did not live there; the Romans ended matters by forbidding the Jews from living in Palestine. Nor could it consist in offering sacrifices in the Temple, which had been destroyed. The people no longer had a principle of identity. What remained was a way of life, whose political, moral, and domestic rules had been formulated by the Torah. This is the meaning of the suffix "-ism" in Judaism. Judaism consists in conducting oneself as if in the land of Judah (the region of Jerusalem), by focusing upon the Torah, by following its rules. The Torah itself was interpreted as a rule of life; this is the meaning of the Hebrew word *halakha* which signifies the path to follow, the "way to conduct one's life."

Judaism is therefore a religion of a book in an entirely different sense than was the religion of ancient Israel, which rested on the political, economic, and cultural life of a nation, a nation which produced a book. Judaism is almost entirely different: it is the book which produced the nation. According to the expression of Heinrich Heine, the Bible is the "portable homeland" of every Jew.[23] To be a Jew is to follow the rules of the Torah, which constitute the deepest identity of a people and which, therefore, require ever more precise specification. To it were added, therefore, discussions concerning the manner of precisely interpreting the commandments and the prohibitions given by God; this formed the Talmud.

b) Christianity

Christianity is first of all a fact, a movement, an event tied to the specific person of Jesus of Nazareth; the book was posterior. When the evangelists recounted the history of Jesus, their aim was not to write a biography but to show that the life of Jesus of Nazareth completed the meaning of the history of Israel, and even of human life as such. The beginning of Christianity was therefore first of all an event: the preaching of Jesus and the proclamation of his disciples who said that he was resurrected, that he appeared to a certain number of witnesses, and that he would return in glory.

The first Christians may have thought that the return of Jesus was near, that Jesus was going to manifest himself soon. They had neither the time nor the need to write this message. At most, one

---

23 H. Heine, *Geständnisse* [1854], in *Werke*, v. 4: *Schriften über Deutschland*, ed. H. Schanze (Frankfort, Insel, 1968), p. 511.

could write to the community to whom one had preached this extraordinary event, to ask it to wait patiently, not to lose hope. This is the content of the oldest texts of the New Testament, the two letters of St. Paul to the Christians of Thessalonica. It was only in a second stage that they began to collect the saying of Jesus, which contained rather remarkable expressions. It seems that they established lists of sayings, as well as of miracles, to which the four evangelists had access, and that these were combined with a historical framework, in order to produce the Gospels from these two sources.

We, therefore, have an event which is recounted afterwards in a book, but the essential was the event, not the book.

c) Islam

Islam is also an event: the first fact of Islamic history that we know by independent, identifiable sources is the seventh-century conquest by Arab tribes of the southern Mediterranean and of the Middle East to Iran. The origin of this expansion seems to be the preaching of an exceptional leader who succeeded in allying these tribes by inaugurating a conquest, perhaps of the entire world, of a vast territory in any event. The sayings of this preacher were collected at a date that can hardly be determined. According to Muslim tradition, Mohammed would have begun receiving messages from above toward 610 or 615. After having preached to his compatriots of Mecca without great success, around 622 he went to Medina, where he received a better welcome. He then would have returned with a force to Mecca a short while before his death in 632.

We do not know exactly when the Quran was brought together.[24] According to the dominant tradition, it would have been the third successor of Mohammed, Osman (*Uthmân*), caliph from 644 to 656, who established a unified text. He would have had a certain

---

24 See A. -L. de Prémare, *Les Fondations de l'islam. Entre écriture et histoire* (Paris, Le Seuil, 2002) and his excellent little book, *Aux origines du Coran. Questions d'hier, approches d'aujourd'hui* (Paris, Téraèdre, 2004).

number of copies made in order to send to the principal centers of the Arab army; he would have had other texts burned, which explains why there is only one, the deviant sources having been destroyed. Western scholars do not accept this version of the facts for various reasons, including contradictions in the narratives. They themselves, however, have arrived at contradictory conclusions.

The book plays in Islam, as a mode of life producing a civilization, a special place. It was necessary to give rules of life to all these conquerors of an immense territory, so that they could distinguish themselves from others. These rules were sought in the Quran. There they found certain rules attributed to God himself, for example, concerning questions of inheritance, of marriage, of penal law. This however amounted to very little. They, therefore, were completed by declarations of the prophet, real or supposed, which became the source of law. What Mohammed, the perfect man, did, the Muslim ought to be able to do also, unless the text specifies that something was a privilege of the Prophet (e.g., Quran, XXXIII, 50).

4. *The idea of revelation*

The concept of "revealed religion" is also deceptive, because "revelation" does not have the same meaning in the three religions.

What is revealed in Judaism is the history of the people of Israel. This history is more than the indifferent context within which something of God would have been revealed. The events themselves are at once the means of revelation and its object. The commands contained in the Torah were given by God at a certain moment in this history. Among them, which were directly revealed? The rabbis discussed the question: The entire Torah? The Ten Commandments? Solely the Name of God, all the rest having been uttered by Moses?

For Christianity, the revealed object is not the New Testament, but the person of Christ himself; the book only recounts the history, reports the teaching, of this person.

In Islam, the revealed object is truly the book; the person of Mohammed, at least in primitive Islam, had little importance.

This is why one can consider Islam to be the sole religion of the book in the strict sense. For Islam, the Quran has for its author not Mohammed but God who dictated it to him; Mohammed was merely the scribe. In the same way, the author of *Paradise Lost* was Milton, not the daughter to whom, having become blind, he dictated his poem.

In Judaism and Christianity, the holy book is an inspired book, that is to say, written and composed by men who are "aided" by God, in such a way that they do not teach any errors concerning his nature or his will. But nothing prevents the Bible from containing errors of fact, for example, in matters of chronology, nor that it contains a vision of the physical universe that today is completely passé. For Islam, the Quran *cannot* contain error, contradiction, or supersedable content. What seems to be so is rectified in passages that are assumed to have been subsequently revealed. It is necessary that everything in the Quran be true, even definitive. That is why an abundant, and regularly revised, literature attempts to show, with each new scientific discovery, that it was contained in the Quran.

If the revealed *objects* differ, the revealed *content* of these objects differs as well. For Judaism and Christianity, revelation is a self-manifestation of God by himself. A manifestation of God which, because it is personal, necessarily remains mysterious. For Islam, God does not manifest himself as he is in himself, but only expresses his will in uttering commands. And there is no question of him entering into human history by contracting an alliance with man.

Thus, the presence of a book, a fact common to all three religions, masks three different ways of relating to that book. These, in turn, flow from the three different ideas of the way in which these sacred books were communicated to men.

IV. Three religions?

One can extend these observations with an even more provocative question. Is it the case that *three* religions really exist?

1. How do the three religions distinguish themselves from each other?

Let us begin with Christianity. It is a form of Judaism. Jesus of Nazareth was a Jew, the twelve apostles as well, as was St. Paul and the other authors of the New Testament. Christianity began as a sort of Jewish history, then it gradually, and painfully, separated itself from Judaism. On the one hand, because Christians – those who followed St. Paul – turned to the pagans to announce the good news of the resurrection. On the other hand, because the Jews considered the Christians to be heretics, and excluded them from the community. A tension emerged which ended with the gradual separation of the two religions, but from an initial unity.

Islam in contrast was born independently of Israël, far from the Holy Land, and among a people that was not Jewish. Mohammed was neither Jewish nor Christian. According to traditional history, he was rebuffed by the rabbis of Medina, who refused to recognize his message. This is why he "theorized" this difference, by claiming, as we saw, a connection with Abraham prior to the law of Moses and the life of Jesus.

Three religions therefore, or two? In a certain way, one can consider that we are in the presence of two "demi-religions," on one hand, Judaism and the Christian rending of Jewish unity, and on the other, a religion, Islam, which one can consider, depending upon one's view, as a second, or third, religion.

2. Three books?

The answer to this question is not simple because Christianity has a "double" holy book which includes the holy book of Judaism. The expression "the Bible" merits attention. To say "the Old and the New Testament" seems obvious. However, to retain the Old Testament was not obvious; during the second century C.E. primitive Christianity was tempted to discard the Old Testament. This was the endeavor of Marcion. For him, the God of the Old Alliance was a God of wrath, who was supplanted by the God of love of the Gospel.[25] The Church did not follow this path, however, considering Marcion to be a heretic; it retained the paradox of a double holy book. Judaism and Christianity therefore have in common the Old Testament. The New Testament constitutes the way in which Christians interpret the events of the life of Jesus in the light of what had been announced, at least according to them, in the Old Testament.

Islam in contrast has a holy book that is proper to it. It is not understood as a sort of "Third Testament." In fact, as we have seen, it is a fundamental teaching of Islam, without which it probably could not exist, that the books appealed to currently by the other two religions are not genuine. Islam, therefore, has no need of either the Old or the New Testament. In practice, it does not read them, sometimes it even forbids their being read.

We have already observed that two-and-a half religions, rather than three, exist. In the same way we have two-and-a half books rather than three, with the difference between Judaism and Christianity residing, rather naturally, in the reading given of the Old Testament, quite different in the two religions.

Conclusion

The use of the three expressions I just studied arises, to be sure, from the best will in the world. People seek to discern the common elements upon which they are all agreed, in order to make possible a productive dialogue. However, we know where good intentions often lead. In fact, the vocabulary I criticized gives rise to confusions rather than clarity. It masks real differences underneath a surface harmony. As a result, it produces the opposite of what it desires. If one wants to have a real dialogue, one must begin by respecting the other. This implies that one understand

25 See the great book – finally available in French (even though it was published in 1924) – of A. von Harnack, *Marcion: The Gospel of the Alien God* (Wipf & Stock Publishers, 2007).

him as he understands himself, taking the words he uses with the meaning he gives them, and accepting the initial situation of disagreement, in order to move forward toward better understanding.

Chapter 2
To Know God

Once we have established the diversity of the three religions, and we have recognized the central place of the idea of God in each, we can undertake the study of the way in which one of them, Christianity, takes up the question of God, and first of all, the question of how to gain access to God. How can we "know" God? Before such a question, let us begin by becoming aware of the way in which it is usually posed. Most often we suppose that knowing is an activity that, at bottom, is not problematic. On the other hand, we believe that what is difficult is to know how to bring this activity to bear upon a very particular object, to wit: God.

Now, we either do not, or poorly, know God. But there is at least one thing that we know well, which is knowledge itself. Because of this we know what "to know" means. In general, scientific knowledge has, since the seventeenth century, furnished us with the model of real knowledge. It began with the emergence of the mathematical sciences of nature, with Galileo's physics in particular, then the sciences of biology or economics, thus providing the model of reliable knowledge. All that remains is to apply this to a determinate object.

This is what we *believe* we do. But if we look closer, this is not at all what we *actually are doing*. In fact, we naturally distinguish several ways of knowing.

I. To know

1. What does "to know" mean?
The French language distinguishes "savoir" and "connaître," as do other languages but not English, which always uses "to know."

One can say: "savoir" is always about predicates, while "connaître" means to know the thing. In the first case, we say "I know *that* . . . such-and-such is the case with the thing"; for example, that the sky is blue. In contrast, one uses "connaître" with a direct object, although in very different instances. One can know Paris, know a science, know a person. Even, as with the title of this chapter, know God.

However, in the final analysis, it does not often happen that we use "know" with a direct object. Or, when we do, it is not the case that what we know is always directly the object. Thus, to know Paris can mean that one knows the history of the city and its neighborhoods. But most times it means to be able to get around, to find stores and metro stops. Sometimes it means to know how to conduct oneself, the informal code of conduct that allows one not to be inappropriate and to attain one's ends. To know in this case means to know how to manage, how to get along.

Now, the first way of doing so involves putting something in a class, a category. This is why "to know" often means "to recognize": I recognize this car, meaning: I know its make and model, and I can list its characteristics. In the case of the computer upon which I am typing right now, to say that I know it can mean either 1) to know how to use it; or 2) to know the scientific and engineering laws according to which the information is transmitted, in other words, computer science. In the two cases, it isn't really the particular object that I know, but a genus. I, a simple user of the computer, know how to use a certain kind of computer; the computer technician knows the laws that would allow him, as need be, to repair or construct such a machine.

The two, however, do not necessarily imply one another. To know how to play a certain card game, you have to know the rules. But that is not sufficient, you also have to have a certain sense or feel that only practice can give you. On the other hand, one can speak and write a language perfectly well, without knowing all its rules. I still remember, for example, my surprise when I was told as a very young person that there was a rule that I was unwittingly applying, which required the use of the subjunctive after superlatives or adjectives like "the first, the last."

From all this, we can see that the various types of knowledge range themselves along an axis that goes between the two poles of "savoir" and "connaître." And both, in a way that may surprise, emerge more from the domain of practice than of a knowledge that one would consider to be pure theory or contemplation. Practice in turn divides into the two domains that Aristotle already distinguished: on one hand, fabrication (*poièsis*), where we produce an object that is external to our activity; on the other hand, action properly speaking (*praxis*), in which one "does" nothing other than the action itself, for example, when one performs in a play.[1] In this way, "connaître" means either to be able to utilize or to be able to (re)produce. In other words, it means either knowing how to do something with a thing or how one can construct it. In neither case does the knowledge directly bear upon the thing.

2. To know the singular

There is but one case in which we know things themselves, and therefore in which the use of the verb "to know" with a direct object is not only customary in ordinary language but legitimate for philosophical reflection. This is when things are singular, unique. However, upon reflection, it is not so easy to find things that are unique.

Let us begin with *objects*, and look at the circumstances where we move from the indefinite article "a/an" to the definite article "the." This hat is *a* hat. But it is *the* hat of Napoleon, that is, of a singular person, the one he wore during the battle of Austerlitz, itself a singular event. More modestly, this pen becomes, as it were, singularized, because it is *my* pen, the one I used to write this particular letter, the one I eventually chewed on while thinking. It is the presence of a person, whether actual or passed, that singularizes an object. This is why an object is never better

---

1   Aristotle, *Nicomachean Ethics*, VI, 5, 1140b6–7.

singularized than in the case of a work of art. It often bears the signature of its creator; in any event, it bears the trace of his style.

What about *events*? They are singular in the measure that they receive dates. Let's take the example of an eclipse. It occurs according to certain immutable laws. As such, it isn't an event, but an astronomical occurrence that one can predict in advance. In a certain sense, it is something that recurs. An eclipse is not singular, and only becomes an event when it is dated. Dated relative to what? Not to another physical occurrence. To be sure, dates depend upon a series of physical processes, a certain number of rotations of the earth or solar revolutions emanating from an original event, itself a solar revolution among others. But the date does not become pertinent until it is situated vis-à-vis human facts, for example, in western civilization the birth of Christ. An event is historical in the measure that it is placed in a context that gives it human meaning.

A "thing" therefore is not capable of supporting on its own the weight of singularity. It receives what singularizes it from elsewhere, from events and, ultimately, from persons. This is what allows the distinction between *experimentation* and *experience*.

By definition, an experiment is repeatable, because we decide to ignore the circumstances that make it unique; these include the date, the name of the scientist, and the place of the experiment. Paul Valéry wrote: "How many things we have to ignore, in order to act!"[2] One must also say, "How many things we have to ignore, in order to know!" As needed, we isolate the thing we experiment with, not only in thought, but also in a quite concrete way: by enclosing it in a calorimeter, or in a black box, eventually we put it in orbit in order to remove it from heat, light, and weight.

Experience, in contrast, is always unique, and precisely because instances line up, they can be added and come to form "the experience" of a person who "has" experience. This is true because the life of a human person is, in a preeminent way,

2 P. Valéry, *Tel Quel*, "Choses tues," in *Oeuvres*, ed. J. Hytier (Paris, Gallimard, 1960), t. 2, p. 503.

non-repeatable. Our life forms a whole: unified by memory, the self makes (in Bergson's famous image) a snowball of itself.[3] What happens to me becomes part of me, I can never bring it about that it did not happen to me. It is only a manner of speaking to say, "I began from ground zero." The single person as such will never know what it is to be married, the married man will never know what it is to remain single. One cannot, strictly speaking, choose among the various possibilities that are on the same plane. For example, "to experience" several women before choosing "the right one" may be morally blameable. But above all, and before that, it is quite simply impossible. One cannot compare: after having lived with one woman, lady X, I am no longer the same, such that I would be able to repeat the experience with the next one, lady Y.

3. Self-knowledge, personal knowledge, knowledge of God

Let us consider therefore what knowledge of persons is. I will begin with what seems to be the closest to it, our self-knowledge.

Do we know ourselves? You recall the inscription that was etched on the entrance to the temple dedicated to Apollo at Delphi: "Know thyself!" Its original meaning was probably an invitation to follow measure, in keeping with the spirit of the local god: "Know that you are but a man!" Socrates took it as his motto, and gave it a different sense. Now, in a certain way this counsel fulfills itself, as I will indicate in a moment. Certainly, we are a mystery to ourselves. Only think of the abysses of memory, or of what is called depth-psychology. But one also has to note a paradox, one that St. Augustine brought to light. Even if we are incapable of making an exhaustive inventory of what we contain, in any case we know *where* we have to search.[4] As soon as we understand the injunction of the god at Delphi, we show that we know ourselves, since we at least understood to *whom* it is addressed.

3 H. Bergson, *Essai sur les données immédiates de la conscience*, III.
4 St. Augustine, *De la Trinité*, X, III, 5 (Bibliothèque augustinienne, Desclée de Brouwer, 1994), t. 16, pp. 128–30.

And other persons? Can we truly say that we *know* them? Especially those whom we love? If "know" means to know the physical, biological, and other laws that govern them, it would not be as persons that we know them, but as specimens of a determinate species. To know a person most often means: know how to identify her and, beyond her name, know how to treat her. This "to treat her," of course, does not mean "utilize," but to conduct oneself in the light of the age, sex, social rank, profession, and opinions of the other. But if "know" is taken to mean "know how to manipulate," then we no longer are treating them as persons, but as instruments.

Here it is important to determine properly the class of objects within which we are going to place God. Should we consider him as a *thing* or as a *person*? Too often, we are inclined to place him among things, even if a thing of a very particular nature, accessible to the reasoning of the intellect rather than the grasp of perception. In this connection, many philosophers give the impression that they see in the existence and attributes of God facts that one can describe without further ado. Spinoza wrote at the end of the first part of the *Ethics*: "In what preceded, I explained the nature and properties of God"; or Hegel characterizes his logic as "the presentation (*Darstellung*) of God as He is in his eternal essence before the creation of nature and of finite spirit."[5] In saying this, I am not contenting myself with a naïve reading of these two philosophers, who were anything but naïve. However, these formulas betray a certain lack of prudence on the part of philosophers that one, perhaps paradoxically, encounters less frequently among theologians.

For Christianity, God is something like a person. This obviously does not mean that he is a man. Here I feel the need to be precise because too often "person" and "man" or "human" are

---

5   B. Spinoza, *Ethica ordine geometrico demonstrata*, I, Appendice, "Opera quotquot reperta sunt," ed. J. Van Vloten and J. P. N. Land (La Haye, Nijhoff, 1914 (3rd ed.), t. 1, p. 66; G. W. F. Hegel, *Wissenschaft der Logik*, "Allgemeiner Begriff der Logik," ed. G. Lasson (Hamburg, Meiner, 1967), t. 1, p. 31.

confused. Boethius, however, defined the person, for the first time, as "an individual substance of a rational nature," whatever its nature might be: man, angel, God.[6] It would be better to say more precisely that God is superpersonal. But here too, a danger lurks: one runs the risk of thinking that this means *im*personal, while it would be more exact to say that he is *more personal* than the persons we are familiar with. In any case, he resembles a person more than a material object.

One can have an idea of this by considering the famous response given to Moses: "I am [will be] who I am [will be]." (*Exodus* 3, 14). At first glance, one can see in these words a refusal to answer, like children who exempt themselves from answering by saying, "because, because." Whoever speaks Hebrew today will understand it in that way. But more deeply it is a real response, one that is very precise, perfectly adequate to its object. In truth, of a person, of a living freedom, one can rightly say – and one cannot say of anything else – he will be what he will be.

When we ask someone, who are you?, most often we want to ask, what is your name? Or: What is your profession? Or again: Why are you here? What are you doing here? But when the question is genuine and deep, when it corresponds to a desire to know the person as such, the only true response is: "You will see. . . ." Moreover, it cannot be given except in an experience rooted in love or friendship. Love consists precisely in the space that is opened, in which the other person can say, or rather, show, what he or she is. Or rather: what he or she *will be*.

4. To look in the right place

Now, the attitude that culminates in love – allowing the other to be what he "wants" to be – is found at all levels of knowledge. Let us take up a classic distinction, made famous by Husserl, between two kinds of phenomena: 1) those that are immediately

6 Boethius, *Against Eutyches*, 3, in *The Theological Tractates*, ed. H. F. Stewart et al. (Cambridge, Mass., Harvard University Press, 1973), p. 84.

given in the experience I have of myself; call them "immanent." 2) Those that I receive from elsewhere; these are called "transcendent" phenomena.[7] "Inner experiences" (*Erlebnis*) are immanent, things (*Ding*) are transcendent. "Things" in this case means everything not given in an immediate experience of ourselves. In this sense, material objects are things, but so are mathematical laws, animals, men, angels (if they exist), and even God, are also "things."

Let us articulate a rule that seems obvious, but whose implications go very far. In order to know "things," since they are "outside," one has to go seek them, and seek them *where they are*. The "where they are" is sometimes relatively simple: to see colors, it suffices to turn on a light and open one's eyes. But it is sometimes more complicated. To see a train pass, one has to be alongside railway tracks; to see koala bears, one probably has to go to Australia; to know what inebriation is, one has to drink alcohol in sufficient quantities; to see microbes, you need a microscope. In the case of certain realities that are hard to access, you need a special strategy in order, as the phrase has it, "to put them into evidence": devise an experimental process, special measuring instruments, often an entire rather complicated apparatus. And contrary to what the etymology of the word "evidence" suggests (it comes from the word "videre," to see), this evidence is not always able to be seen with the eyes of the body. One can deduce the existence of a particle from its effects, or reconstruct the ancestor of an animal species when there are no fossil remains by taking one's bearings from still existing animals, or move from a surface phantasm to its cause in psychoanalysis. Not without some uncertainly, to be sure.

From these observations one can derive the following rule: in each case, *it is the nature of the object that dictates to me the way I am to gain access to it.* This even begins with perception. Each sense

7   E. Husserl, *Ideen zu einer reinen Phänomenologie und phänomenologischen Philosophie*, I, #42, ed. W. Biemel (La Haye, Nijhoff, 1950), pp. 95–98.

has a proper object, without this distinction the objects of one sense could overlap with those of another. This was already noted by the Greeks, who saw a philosophical problem in it: how can I perceive one and the same object via the different senses that do not communicate with one another?[8] One can generalize from this: I cannot know colors other than by sight, and equations other than by mathematical reasoning. I cannot summon objects to manifest themselves to me simply as I wish, I cannot ask to hear a color or see a sound. I have to conform myself to their manner of manifestation. Aristotle called the person "cultivated, well-educated" (*pepaideumenos*) who knew what type of approach belonged to each object. I cannot demonstrate a moral judgment with the mathematical form A + B; conversely, I cannot persuade anyone simply by rhetorical techniques of the probability of a geometrical theorem.[9]

To ignore this rule leads to gross stupidities. For example, Cabanis's misguided utterance: "The soul? For thirty years I have dissected corpses, and I have never encountered it." He was a great doctor, perhaps, but this declaration was simply silly. He sought the soul precisely where it was not. There was nothing surprising that he could not find it in an in-animated body: by definition, it is deprived of a soul (*anima*). We can also refer to those misguided minds who draw their watches and challenge God to strike them with lightning in less than five minutes.[10] The god who would respond to this challenge, would it be God? It would even be an insult to the ancients Greeks to think this of Zeus. God knows how to save, not damn. As for the idea of summoning God to manifest himself, Giraudoux said the essential in a scene of a comedy: a person who does not believe in "spirits" orders them to do miracles on command; they do so, promptly and effectively – but the one who demanded them

8   See Gorgias, *On non-being*, DK 82B3, #83–4, t. 2, p. 282; Aristophanes, *Thesmophoriazusai*, 5–11; Sextus Empiricus, *Hypotyposes*, I, xiv, 91–4; St. Augustine, *Confessions*, X, vii, 11, BA, t. 14, p. 160.

9   Aristotle, *Nichomachean Ethics*, I, 3, 1094b23–1095a2.

10 A. de Musset, *La Confession d'un enfant du siècle*, I, 2, ed. D. Leuwers (Paris, GF-Flammarion, 1993), p. 39.

immediately finds a natural cause for them![11] This is as smart as saying, "I haven't botched a single painting exhibition in thirty years, why then all the buzz around Mozart?" What is irksome is that many men reason this way, if one can call it "reasoning."

II. A particular object

1. "Open your eye, the good eye!"

How then to know God? We begin with a sentence from the American philosopher and mathematician, C. S. Peirce: "To see God, if suffices to open one's eyes, and one's heart, which is also an organ of perception."[12] This, of course, does not mean that the knowledge of God belongs to the order of sensation, as it is different from other faculties, such as the intellect. If, therefore, to know God it suffices "to open the eye, and the good eye," what is this *good eye* one must open? And how is the heart an organ of perception? A phrase from Pascal comes to everyone's memory: "God [who is] accessible to the heart, not reason . . . ." A similar caveat is in order: this in no way means, as is often said: accessible to sentimentality. To be persuaded, read another aphorism: "The heart senses that there are three dimensions in space and that numbers are infinite."[13] One is a thousand miles from sentimentality. Pascal means that there is an organ for knowing God that perceives him in an original way, just as there is a faculty of the soul by which we give our assent to the principles of mathematical reasoning, and which is not to be confused with the other faculty, i.e., reason, which allows us to deduce from them the demonstration of the various theorems.

Is there, then, a "sense of God" like there is a sense of color? A sense that would be faith? The phrase "sense of God" seems to be

11 J. Giraudoux, *Intermezzo*, Act I, scene 4.
12 C. S. Peirce, *Philosophical Writings*, ed. J. Buchler (New York, Dover, 1955), pp. 377–78.
13 Pascal, *Pensées*, ed. L. Brunschvicg, IV, #278 (Paris, Hachette, 1924), t. 2, p. 201; then #282, p. 204. Cf. J. Laporte, *Le Coeur et la Raison selon Pascal* (Paris, Elzévir, 1950).

not wholly devoid of truth, but it requires a certain delicateness of thought, because the vocabulary of "sense" almost necessarily gives rise to the idea of something "irrational," something incommunicable, even arbitrary. Hence, two dangers. First, to take "religion" as "religiosity," founded upon a "religious sentiment"; we have increasingly used this phrase ever since its invention in the nineteenth century.[14] The second danger is worse, and is as old as humanity itself. It is to seek to produce these sensations and experiences of the divine in ecstatic worship. This, however, is magic, not religion. Magic consists in treating God as a useable object, one subject to technique, and not as a person. Contrary to what is often thought, magic is not at all allied to religion. Nothing in fact is farther removed.

This leads me to a distinction also made by Pascal. His thought is often summarized, in the aphorisms where he talks about clarity and obscurity, by saying that God hides himself so that we can retain our freedom of choice. A facile success is thus assured, as one says with a dramatic tone in one's voice, that a loving father nonetheless does not fail to assist his children, leaving traces of himself, and so forth. This is perfectly – and banally – true, and beside the point. The real Pascal was much more complex. I will only comment on one formulation: "He [God] hides himself from those who tempt him, and he reveals himself to those who seek him."[15] This does not mean that God punishes those who tempt him and rewards those who seek him. This, if I can put it this way, is not his *modus operandi*. What Pascal really means is that "tempting" God is not the right way to seek him, it's the wrong "method." In his way, Pascal applies to the knowledge of God a rule analogous to that of Aristotle discussed earlier, which requires that one respects the way that objects give themselves to us. This rule also inspires the ideal Pascal calls "the honorable man." While the specialist considers the world through his particular angle, be he a geometer or a military strategist, the honorable

14 See F. Schleiermacher, *Über die Religion. Reden an die Gebildeten unter ihren Verächtern*, 2.
15 *Pensées*, #557, *op. cit*, t. 3, p. 7.

man takes me as I am.[16] The believer is the one who applies to God the rule of knowing how to live rightly used by the well-bred man vis-à-vis his interlocutors.

"To tempt" God is to apply to him a kind of experimental method, to summon him and require that he manifest himself in conditions imposed by the summoner, without asking if these are truly appropriate. "To seek" God, on the other hand, is to go to seek him where he is. In other words, it is to convert, or turn oneself, in the original Platonic sense of "turning oneself in the right direction."[17] This is not always easy. It is not enough to *say* or to *imagine* that one is seeking God, to be truly seeking him. Pascal, again, puts us on guard against this error: "Men often take their imagination for their heart; and they believe that they have converted as soon as they think of converting."[18] On the other hand, if one truly seeks God, that is, where he is, the basic rule is reassuring and is found in the Gospel itself: "He who seeks, finds." (*Matthew*, 7, 8).

2. *Faith and knowledge*

The distinction often made between belief and faith can be taken up at this point. Belief is an imperfect knowledge of what can be known; it is a "for-want-of-better" vis-à-vis knowledge. In my bed in the morning, I believe it is nice outside, because the wheels of passing cars do not make the sound they do when it is raining. But I simply have to poke my nose out the door to *know* that it is nice. In that case, it makes no sense to say that "I believe" it is nice.

On another hand, belief can be the most perfect knowledge that is available because it pertains to an object that can only be imperfectly known. In other words, it is imperfect because its object is. I *believe* that it will be nice tomorrow, because tomorrow's weather is unknown. To be sure, it can happen that in itself the future is determined in some necessary fashion and (according to Laplace's dream, is) foreseeable; but as an object of my

16 Id., #36, t. 1, p. 46.
17 Plato, *Republic*, VII, 521c6.
18 Pascal, *Pensées*, #275, *op. cit.*, t. 2, p. 200.

knowledge it is not. In the first case, the state of things believed is present, in the second, it belongs to the future. But from the point of view of the knowing subject, the two cases are the same; they're half-way knowledge. It only would take me a few seconds in the first case, twenty four hours in the second, to come to know.

Here we need to introduce yet another distinction. One can "believe something," but one can also "believe someone," even going so far as "to believe in someone." I can believe that it is raining outside. This belief is susceptible to different degrees of certainty, for example, according to whether I hear the rain beating against my shutters or only hear the tires on the road outside sound wet. As a consequence, the assent, and the behavior that follows from it, will themselves be relative to the indices upon which the belief is based. I will bring my umbrella in the first case, open my windows to check things out in the second. Here enters a rule that John Locke articulated in the seventeenth century to guard against "enthusiasm": to grant one's belief only in the exact measure that arguments, signs, or witnesses guarantee it. Every "surplusage of assurance" would come not from a true love of the truth, but from the excess of passion.[19] Of course, in practice this rule, which seems to be simple and reasonable, is not so easy to apply.[20]

If "to believe something" is susceptible of degrees, "to believe someone" is not. You cannot have partial confidence in a person. Or if one does, to that extent you have ceased considering him as a full person. None of this entails that the content of this full confidence cannot vary, and be understood in a number of ways. For example, when a father says to his son that he is taking him "to someone who will help him," the son might think it is to a candy store, while the father has in mind the dentist. The child in other words can mistake his father's words and yet still have full confidence in his dad, that he intends to tell him the truth. Let us

19 J. Locke, *An Essay concerning Human Understanding*, IV, chapter 29, #1, ed. J. Yolton (London, Everyman, 1964), t. 2, p. 288.

20 See the discussion in J. H. Newman, *An Essay in Aid of a Grammar of Assent* [1870] (Notre Dame, Ind.: University of Notre Dame Press, 2003), pp. 138–39.

apply this principle, analogously, to the idea of the God whom Christianity, following the Old Testament, gives the name of "Father." One can then say that the believer is convinced that this God wills his good – and not (a preposterous formula) His own good. But this does not entail that he understands in what this good consists.

In the case of God, faith bears simultaneously upon a content and the one who reveals it. More specifically, in Christianity the content of Revelation is nothing other than the one who reveals himself, and not, for example, a will that reveals nothing about the revealer.

3. To know a paradoxical object

Faith is the knowledge adequate to a paradoxical "object." Of this object, God, one can say in all truth that he is "hidden" (*mistattèr*), according to the often-cited phrase of the prophet Isaiah, which has become quasi-proverbial in the Latin form given it in the Vulgate Bible: *Deus absconditus* (*Isaiah*, 45, 15).[21] But it is equally true to say that he is manifest. Everything depends upon knowing *to what* he is hidden, and *to what* he is manifest.

One often hears that God is mysterious. Too often what is meant by that is that he refuses our efforts at coming to grips with him. Or worse, that to approach him would require launching oneself in the dark waters of occult experiences. Or worst of all, that we have to swallow without any thought whatever is said by those who claim to speak in his name. In truth, though, mystery is a daily experience, one that could almost be called normal. Each day we encounter mysterious beings, unfathomable beings whom we will never plumb. Every person, because he is free, represents this sort of mystery. Who has ever heard it said that someone has completely come to know even those he knows best: his spouse, his children, his friends? In my case, it is now forty years that I do *not* know my wife.

21 On the probable original meaning, see C. R. North, *The Second Isaiah, Introduction, Translation and Commentary of the Chapters XL-LV* (Oxford, Clarendon Press, 1964), pp. 138–39.

It would be better to say: God is hidden because he is only accessible to faith. God is hidden from those ways of knowing that nonetheless function very well where, precisely, it is not a question of God, but of something else: colors, equations, or men. Faith knows God as hidden. But to faith he truly reveals himself. This obviously does not mean that God would not exist without faith, as if faith created its object.

In this way the distinction between faith and "savoir-knowledge" loses its definitive status. A glance at the texts of St. Paul which constitute the *loci classici* of this distinction shows that his teaching is more complex than is usually thought. Paul distinguishes two ways of "walking": "we walk (*peripatein*) by faith (*pistis*), not by *eidos*" (2 *Corinthians*, 5, 7). The word I left in Greek (*eidos*) is often translated as "clear vision." This word first of all refers to the human form, that which makes personality visible, hence, in first place, one's face or visage. The focus upon the face suggests that it is a matter of personal knowledge, not the comprehension of a thing.

If the terms of the opposition are complex, the opposition itself is. It is too simple to say that knowledge will replace faith, which will fall away. Because Paul also says that, different from charity which will never cease, "knowledge" itself "will pass away" (1 *Corinthians*, 13, 8). Moreover, Paul does not starkly oppose faith and knowledge; he also opposes two forms of knowledge: "At present, I know (*ginôskô*) in part; then I will know (*epignôsomai*) as I am known" (ibid., 13, 12). In this way, the first type of knowledge corresponds to what he elsewhere calls "faith." Elsewhere, finally, to know God and to be known by him are not relegated to the future, but both are put in the present: "Now that you know God, or rather, that you are known by him" (*Galatians*, 4, 9).

4. Faith, will, love

The formula in which Paul reverses the relationship between the subject and object of knowledge, "to know as one is known," implies the abandonment of the attitude of mastery vis-à-vis the object. This returns us to the practical dimension of knowledge, where to know something is to be able to do something with it. Once I know something, I have to ask, what purpose does the knowledge serve? What do we want to do with God once we know him? But if we were able to do something with him, this would not be God. In a sense, knowledge of God is useless. To be sure, no more or less useless than everything that is not a means for obtaining something else, but an end in itself. This is true of the practices that are the most interesting for human life, which include art, science, moral life, all the "liberal" activities, those that are worthy of a free man. In contrast, and by definition, everything that serves is servile.

Let us articulate yet another rule: God does not refuse whatever a being needs. But one has to specify: needs *in order to do what*? To achieve its good. He gives the mineral the existence that immediately coincides with its good. To the plant, what it needs to grow and to reproduce, to the animal what it needs to feed itself, to capture its prey, to attract its sexual partner. The God who gives the good thus presents himself differently, but analogously, according to the level of nature in question, be it the mineral, the living, or the human order. To be sure, "the idea of God has no meaning unless their unification occurs and, above all, unless it is professed by men."[22]

What, then, is our good? I emphasize "our" good, what concerns us insofar as we are genuinely ourselves, rational and free subjects. Not simply our good insofar as we are living beings, whose good is life, nor even insofar as we are intelligent beings whose good is happiness. God does not seek our happiness. He does not seek our unhappiness either. He seeks our *good*, which is to say: our sanctification. "Be ye holy as I am holy," said the God of the Old Testament (*Leviticus,* 17). Our good, in other words, is God himself. "It is good for me to adhere to God" (*Mihi adhaerere Deo bonum est*), as we find in Psalm 72, so often cited by St. Augustine.[23]

22 B. Saint-Sernin, *Le rationalisme qui vient* (Paris, Gallimard, 2007), p. 130.

23 E.g., St. Augustine, *De moribus ecclesiae catholicae*, I, xvi, 27 (Bibliothèque augustinienne, 1949), t. 1, p. 176.

If God is the good, one can ask if it is even *possible* not to love him. Pascal, whom I have often cited, left us the following enigmatic saying: "How far it is from the knowledge of God to loving him."[24] Is this a thesis awaiting its argument? Or is it a sigh (an editor adds an exclamation point)? In any case, one cannot interpret the saying as if it meant to say that, supposing that we genuinely know God, we would still be able not to love him. As soon as we conceive God as he is, that is, as the Author of all good, we *cannot not* love him.[25] In contrast, what we cannot love, what we have the strictest duty to hate, are the widespread idols which make him a cruel, calculating, petty, even sadistic being.

If God is the Good and if he wills our good, which is our sanctification, what knowledge of God do we need for this sanctification? Precisely that which faith provides, a union of wills with him. Two centuries before Pascal, at the end of the fourteenth century, one reads a phrase from the Florentine humanist Marsilio Ficino that strangely resembles what we just read from Pascal: "God gives himself as a reward to those who love him, rather than those who examine and interrogate him" (*Amantibus . . . Deus se ipsum retribuit potius quam scrutantibus*).[26] It is not a matter of examining God, as though one placed him in a police line-up. This is not out of arbitrary caprice but because, quite simply, it is an inappropriate way. To seek to unmask him (in French, *dé-visager*) would be, quite literally, to deny him the face (*visage*) that makes him a person.

From this, one understands better why the act of faith must be a free act. This is not only so that it can be a meritorious act, but for two reasons. On the one hand, so that it can be an *act*, properly speaking, not something that is automatic, a reflex, a matter of routine. On the other hand, so that it can truly achieve its object. To be sure, one can say, if one wishes, that the act of faith

---

24 Pascal, *Pensées*, #280, *op. cit.*, t. 2, p. 203.
25 Dante, *Divina commedia*, Purgatorio, XVII, 109–11; see St. Thomas's discussion, *Summa theologiae*, II II, q. 34, a. 1.
26 M. Ficino, *Théologie platonicienne de l'immortalité des âmes*, XIV, 10, ed. R. Marcel (Paris, Les Belles Lettres, t. 2, 1964), p. 291.

is meritorious. But what is the reward it "merits"? Nothing other than achieving its object. The recompense of faith is more faith, just as the reward of love is more love.[27] God does not reward love by anything other than love itself.

According to classical theology, that of St. Thomas for instance, the act of faith is an act of will.[28] Once again, this does not mean that one would cause God to exist if one willed very hard. Nor that by willing very hard one would make him visible to something other than the will, in a way that one could retire the will and let him be accessed by another faculty, that of simple observation, for example. By an act of the will one can certainly make images appears and make oneself believe that they have objective reality. But for the accredited spiritual authors, these are idols that one must destroy posthaste.

The will is the organ of the vision of God. The medieval controversies concerning the vision of God which is the joy of the blessed in heaven opposed those, like the Dominicans, who placed the accent on the intellect, and those, like the Franciscans, who underscored the role of the will. According to the former, beatitude consists in "seeing" God; according to the latter, in loving him. But no one ever maintained that the gaze of the blessed could rest upon its divine object without an act of love. This is the case because the faculty which grasps must be of the same nature as the object that is grasped. God being liberty, he can only be encountered in liberty. The act of the will does not occur as a remedy for a defective knowledge, while waiting for better. The beatific vision that we hope for in heaven, and which *is* heaven, is a union in love. We can never do without love.

27 St. John of the Cross, *Cantico espiritual* (B), IX, 7, ed. L. Ruano de la Iglesia (Madrid, BAC, 1989 (12th edition), p. 603.
28 St. Thomas, *De Veritate*, q. 14, a. 3, c.1

Chapter 3
The One God

This God to whom we have access is characterized by a certain number of properties, of "attributes"; I would like to examine a few. I will begin with an attribute that later I will show to be rather particular: unity. The God that the faith of Christians confesses is one God. "One God you will adore" opens the traditional summation of the ten commandments.

I. Oneness

This attribute seems obvious and, like Panisse on his death bed, no one imagines that he has ever sinned against a commandment that is so easy to obey. Seeing this attribute at the beginning of the chapter, we also would say, "Yes, yes, that's true. Agreed. I have never worshiped several gods. . . . Word of honor."[1] However, there can be doubts.

1. The dangers of monotheism

First of all, this is doubtful because of a banal truism: we always have to defend against associating an idol with the one true God, that is, preferring it to him. But more profoundly, is not monotheism itself a sin, even the capital sin? Especially in our day, when "pluralism" benefits from a favorable prejudice. As a result, should not Christians fall in line and declare themselves pluralists? But on what conditions? It is clear that a Christian cannot admit that all truths are equally valid, except at the price of denying his

1   M. Pagnol, *César* [1936] (Paris, Fallois, 2004), p. 22.

own faith. For the Christian, therefore, pluralism can only be the new name given to a reality – itself rather vague – that formerly was called "tolerance." By tolerance is understood the refusal to constrain someone who does not think like us to adhere to what, for us, is the truth.

It is with respect to this that one can ask if Christians can be sincere when they preach tolerance. Did they show themselves tolerant in the past, when they had the power of the majority? In this area, historical arguments prove what they have always proved, which is not much. Examples call forth counter-examples, one ends up with the childish question of "who started it?" In any event, one can always position oneself by ruling out in advance all historical realizations – which are always mixed and impure – of the original message, itself deemed to be pure. At need, one can mask what this retreat into the redoubt of principles can have of awkwardness by means of a comment that is always quite true: Christianity, as with all doctrines, cannot be judged except by the idea it has of the absolute, because it is this idea that in the final analysis (or, in historical language: in the long run) determines the rest.

But doesn't the decisive objection enter precisely at this point? It involves an argument Christians cannot avoid without denying themselves, since it bears upon a fundamental article of their monotheistic faith. The most decided pluralism must admit an exception. And this exception is not a small matter, since it goes to the absolute itself. To acquiesce in pluralism while harboring a reservation about God, is not this equivalent to denying pluralism? In truth, is not monotheism the perfect expression of totalitarianism? Is not the one who professes it irresistibly inclined to refuse to the other his freedom to choose his god and, by the same token, his values, his purpose, his identity? If this is the case, then to profess tolerance can only be an insincere concession. And one would be right to think that, if Christians show themselves to be tolerant, it is because today's circumstances do not favor them, and that only these circumstances prevent an explosion of the fanaticism that monotheism always contains within itself, at least as a seed.

This objection has the merit of requiring us to pose the

problem at a deeper level. As long as one does not examine the Christian conception of the absolute afresh, one will be condemned to remain on the surface. In truth, for the longest time we have been habituated to consider monotheism as intrinsically superior to polytheism. From this point of view, one could either praise Christianity for having maintained the rigor of the prophets' preaching concerning the one God, or blame it for having altered its purity by "associating" two other persons to the one God. In the two cases, however, monotheism would be the uncontested rule for measuring the religious facts.

2. The rediscovery of polytheism

For some time now, however, some have argued that this was nothing but a prejudice, and they have sung the praises of a rediscovered polytheism. The history of this rediscovery up until today would need to be retraced. It did not begin yesterday. Its roots go rather far back into the cultural history of Europe. One, therefore, would have to reconstruct the intellectual climate that made it possible, which ended with a widespread positive reevaluation of paganism, one drawn against the dark image that Christianity had earlier painted. For a long time this tendency was rather diffuse, and stayed at the level of aesthetics. The Renaissance restored meaning to the ancient gods by painting and sculpting them. The German Enlightenment propagated the golden legend of a "serene" (heiter) pagan world, one spared from Christian guilt and anxiety. This is true at its peaks at least, represented by Lessing's monograph on how the Ancients represented death to themselves.[2] The idea according to which Christianity was a "profoundly sad religion, a religion of universal suffering," in which, finally, "beauty" would have been "stricken in heart . . . by the Chimera," was spread through the nineteenth century.[3]

2   G. E. Lessing, *Wie die Alten den Tod gebildet. Eine Untersuchung* [1769], in *Werke* (Munich, Hanser, 1974), t. 4, pp. 405–62.
3   Baudelaire, *Salon de 1846*, IV: E. Delacroix, in *Complete Works*, ed. Y.-G. Le Dantec (Paris, Gallimard, 1961), p. 894; Mallarmé, Letter

Nonetheless, the question of the number of gods was not posed at the outset. To be sure, rediscovered in Florence in the fifteenth century, later neoplatonism gave a certain legitimacy to the Olympic gods by interpreting them in a philosophic manner. Schelling himself integrated a "polytheistic moment" in his construction of monotheism.[4] But it was only with Nietzsche that one found a clear and philosophical statement of the superiority of polytheism to what he mocked as "monotonotheism."[5] However, an adequate discussion of Nietzsche would require a systematic consideration of his entire oeuvre; without this, one would be condemned to ape his own aphoristic style.[6] I will resist the temptation.

Can we still be polytheists? The word, to be sure, has become fashionable among certain intellectuals.[7] These, however, do not attach themselves to its religious character or content, as much as finding in it a tolerant spirit that pleases them. The "gods" in question are hardly anything more than metaphors for "values," as when Weber spoke of the "war of the gods" and he meant conflicting values. One can therefore ask if self-proclaimed polytheists are not secretly monotheists, but monotheists of the human subject. I explain. In their view, only the subject can make gods, and choose among them, determining the number of them as he wishes. All this means that he is better than the gods, that he himself is the sole god.

to Lefébure, 17 May 1867. Earlier, see (in an obviously more positive tone), Chateaubriand, *Génie du christianisme*, II, 3, 9; ed. M. Regard (Paris, Gallimard, 1978), pp. 714–16.

4 F. W. J. Schelling, *Philosophie der Mythologie*, 1st Book: "Der Monotheismus" (Darmstadt, Wissenschaftliche Buchgesellschaft, 1957 [1857], pp. 1–113. The present chapter attempts to draw out some (not always clear) indications from this text.

5 F. Nietzsche, *Götzendämmerung*, "Die "Vernunft"in der Philosophie," #1, KSA, t. 6, p. 75; Der Antichrist, #19, ibid., p. 185.

6 For a good overview, see P. Valadier, *Nietzsche et la critique du christianisme* (Paris, Le Cerf, 1974), pp. 539–51.

7 See, for example, O. Marquard, "Lob des Polytheismus. Uber Monomythie und Polymythie" [1978], in *Zukunft braucht Herkunft. Philosophische Essays* (Reclam, 2003), pp. 46–71.

For me, I have more respect for the "savage" who worships a wooden idol than for the "civilized" person who only bows before himself.

Among the more interesting versions of this tendency, one can cite Jan Assmann, or at least the way some have appealed to the work of this learned Egyptologist, who is equally well-versed in the theory of culture.[8] His essential thesis does not concern the number of divinities, but the "mosaic distinction" which, according to him, would have introduced into religion the distinction between the true and the false, thus inventing the idea of a "false" religion as "idolatry." The response to this of the Protestant theologian Friedrich Wilhelm Graf is that monotheism was even more inventive than this.[9] This rejoinder certainly advances the discussion in the right direction, but it needs to be filled in with more content. This essay is an attempt to do so.

The crudest versions of this tendency today defend Greek polytheism against "Judeo-Christian monotheism." They do so in the name of a pluralism that, sometimes, is not just the flag under which illicit merchandise is smuggled. In this case monotheism is conceived as a particular, but particularly important, case of the denial of plurality and of intolerance. In contrast, polytheism is a particular case of *small is beautiful*. My god is small, but I believe in my god. Or not even, since the "gods" that are affirmed have the good sense not to exist. These rival gods sometimes serve as stand-ins for the claims of independence on the part of different groups, regional autonomy, or the legitimacy of local languages.[10]

8   J. Assmann, *Moses der Ägypter. Entzifferung einer Gedächtnisspur* (Munich, Hanser, 1998), pp. 17–23, 65–66, etc.; *Die mosaische Unterscheidung oder der Preis des Monotheismus* (Munich, Hanser, 2003). Assman corrected many misunderstandings of his thought in a postface to the 3rd edition of his booklet *Politische Theologie zwischen Ägypten und Israel* (Munich, Siemens-Stiftung [not in the bookmarket], 2006, pp. 115–27.

9   F. W. Graf, *Moses Vermächtnis. Über göttliche und menschliche Gesetze* (Munich, Beck, 2006), p. 50; cf. p. 36.

10 See P. Gauthier, "Les illusions du retour à l'Antiquité ou le miroir aux prétextes [. . .]," *Commentaire*, 16, 1981–1982, pp. 584–91.

As an example, recall the invention of a kinder, gentler Catharism, beginning with the television show of Stellio Lorenzi in 1966, *Les Cathares*. The show, produced by a communist and targeted at first against the Catholic Church, later allowed others to use the adjective "Cathar" and apply it not only to regional, but also touristic, and even commercial, purposes. Today it even refers to a cheese, and even to a dish of beans and meat *(cassoulet)*, which raises some suspicion among people who remember that Cathars were vegetarian...

The polemics revolving around monotheism and polytheism do, however, have a healthy aspect. It is the candor with which it avows its hypocrisy and recognizes that its aims are purely political, a domain *(la politique)* that is much more appropriate for such debates than Péguy's other domain, *la mystique*. "Polytheism" becomes a slogan for the claims of particularisms, "monotheism" a slogan for the moral protest of the individual. Both these are fine things, and the task is to connect them with one another. They are so admirable that one regrets seeing them enrolled in the service of a dubious religiosity. Here it is important to recall that it was in the same motion that Christianity, on one hand, rejected religion's contamination of politics and politics' contamination of religion and, on the other, elaborated the conception of God that distinguishes it and without which it would not be itself. I refer to the dogma of the Trinity.

3. *The dogma of the Trinity and political theology*
By confessing the Trinity, orthodox Christianity went well beyond "monotheism" and its various dangers. The merit of having shown that the idea of the Trinity and the rejection of any and all "political theology" go hand-in-hand belongs to the German theologian Erik Peterson, in his small book on the political problem of monotheism.[11] This book appeared at a time and a place that shows

11 E. Peterson, *Der Monotheismus als politisches Problem* (Leipzig, 1935). The work also appeared in *Theologische Traktate* (Munich, Kosel, 1950), pp. 45–147. [Here=*MPP*].

how petty our little debates can be: in Germany in 1935, two years after National Socialism came to power. One heard the affirmations: "One people, one Empire (*Reich*), one Leader (*Führer*)!" Christians confess "one God": do they do so in a similar way to the foregoing? Peterson answered "no!" and took on the notion of "political theology" that had just been rendered popular by the jurist Carl Schmitt.[12] He did so by meditating upon the exemplary, utterly relevant, character of the Arian crisis that had wracked the Church at the beginning of the fourth century. Arianism represented an effort to reconcile monotheism and polytheism. It did so, however, on the model of pagan conceptions, which easily admitted the coexistence of a supreme God and subordinate deities.

For Arianism, the Father was the supreme God and, in a sense, "unique," while the Son was an adoptive divinity. The oneness of the supreme God was conceived in technical terms as his "monarchy," which meant both "a single principle" (*arché*) and "a sole 'prince'" or ruler (*archon*). Hellenistic philosophy thus expressed its conception of the unity of the world by means of categories derived from the political domain. And its decision in favor of a single metaphysical principle came in the last analysis from it.

The same was true, moreover, in the elaboration of the concept of divine monarchy that took place in the Judaism of Alexandria, with Philo of Alexandria. Here it was a matter of justifying the superiority of the Jewish people and its mission vis-à-vis the gentiles. Christian apologists had no difficulty is making use of the argument. And certain pagans, Celsus for example, immediately grasped the political stakes involved, the revolutionary threat posed to the multiethnic Roman Empire.[13] In all this, one has to acknowledge that the initial efforts of Christian theologians to overcome the limitations of the monarchic conception of monotheism were not satisfactory.[14]

For it to be definitively surpassed, its political aspect had to be

12 C. Schmitt, *Politische Theologie* (Munich, 1922).
13 *MPP*, pp. 64, 79–81.
14 Ibid., p. 76.

brought fully to light. This is precisely what happened at the time of the Arian crisis. The emperors maintained a way of looking at the divine that later would be condemned as heretical. In effect it conceived the divine monarchy after the model of the earthly monarchy, in particular, the Roman Empire that dreamed of unifying humanity by bringing the nations into the *pax Romana*. In contrast, the conception that was defined as orthodox recalled that the unity of the human race could only be eschatological. The Church, which is the anticipation of this unification, cannot be confused with the Empire. This way of seeing, therefore, directly threatened the political theology that the imperial court had made its official ideology.[15] The victory of Athanasius over Arianism signified that henceforth one would have to conceive of God and his unity in a way where this unity was *not* the reflection of the earthly monarchy. This meant that the mystery of the Trinity exists only in God, and has no real analogy with the types of unity found within the created world.[16]

The lesson to draw from the Council of Nicea's rejection of a monotheism conceived as a "monarchy" is that one must not conceive God on the model of the created world. In particular, affirming the one God cannot have the same meaning as affirming that a creature, no matter which one, exists as the single instance and exemplar of a class. It does not matter what the single creature is whose unicity serves as the model for thinking the divine unicity. It can be the emperor, conceived as the living icon of the all-powerful. But it can also be the unity of the human race. Or, at the other extreme, it can be the unity of the "I," of the individual subject. Or even of the universe itself, of the whole that exists, by definition, as a *singulare tantum*.

This critique of the application of created models of unity in theology constantly has to be reactivated. One constantly has to show the limits of human models vis-à-vis the unique divine unicity. The seductive models vary according to culture and epoch. Today we are no longer tempted to imagine God after the image

15 Ibid., p. 102.
16 Ibid., p. 103.

of an earthly monarch. But the example of the individual subject is much more tempting in the modern period and no less false. It is to Jürgen Moltmann's credit, therefore, for having extended Peterson's critique, by recalling some old truths about the Trinitarian dogma. In particular he shows the danger involved in speaking of God as an identical subject in three modes of "being" or, in technical terms, of "subsistence." The risk there is to make the three divine Persons only three perspectives on the single God, and thus to fall into the heresy called "modalism." This way of looking unconsciously adopts the modern representation of the individual and naively applies it to God, who is imagined according to the model of the autonomous subject.[17]

Thus, one has to constantly reaffirm the Christian model of the unique God in order to show that it transcends every model of created unicity.

II. Unity

1. "Monotheism": a vague concept

In order to do so, it would be very good to avoid the term "monotheism." It is vague in the extreme. It encompasses the three religions that claim Abraham. But it can also designate, before these, the "primitive monotheism" assumed by the first theoreticians of comparative religion, first proposed by Maimonides, then put back in currency by certain prehistorians.[18] As well as the exclusive worship of the solar disk, Aton, imposed by the Pharaoh Amenophis IV (Akhnaton). The character of this latter monotheism is debated, however. According to the latest scholarship, it is necessary to make some distinctions. Even at the period when the cult of Amon was the object of State persecution, the "heretical"

---

17 J. Moltmann, *Trinität und Reich Gottes. Zur Gotteslehre* (Munich, Kaiser, 1980), above all pp. 144–168 and 207–19.

18 Maimonides, *Mishneh Torah*, "Livre de la connaissance, Idolâtrie," I, 1, ed. M. Hyamson (New York, Feldheim, 1981 [1939]), p. 66a.

Pharaoh was not above associating secondary gods with the worship of the "sole" divinity promulgated by him.[19] The new religions that arose from the Abrahamic religions, or in competition with them, themselves only acknowledge a single god. And even the foregoing list omits several important nuances. For example, the monotheism of Akhnaton is cosmological, while the monotheism of Moses is based upon the historical idea of an exclusive alliance between a people and the unique divinity it agreed to serve.

Moreover, beyond the religious domain, the vision of the world of the Greek philosophers such as Aristotle was decidedly monotheistic. At the culmination of his *Metaphysics*, Aristotle demonstrated the existence of a single principle of movement in the world, as singular as the world itself is, and which he did not hesitate to call "god" (*theos*).[20] The term "monotheism" therefore glosses over what every religion has that is distinctive, for the sake of a poorly defined theism. One is even entitled to ask if the Enlightenment did not use the term precisely for this reason. Or, perhaps, whether it did not arise from the Enlightenment application of the principle of economy, in order to designate the cosmic watchmaker and the policeman of morality in one god. It is clear that a single watchmaker better guarantees the regularity of the world-machine, and a single policeman avoids any conflict of authority and duties.

For all these reasons, it is imperative to examine what Christianity itself says about its God. It confesses a Trinitarian God, a single God in three persons. It is here that we must look. However, because of a lack of space, as well as expertise, it is totally out of the question that I would give a detailed presentation, either of the doctrine itself, or its development. Here I will only recall a few aspects of the teaching in its classic form, aspects that will be chosen in function of the problem we are dealing with.

A single God in three persons: is that a sort of "happy mean" between monotheism and polytheism? As a matter of fact, there is

19 See the recent qualifications in C. Bayer, in *Echnaton, Sonnenhymnen. Ägyptisch / Deutsch* (Stuttgart, Reclam, 2007), pp. 55–56.
20 Aristotle, *Metaphysics*, XII, 7, 1072b25, 29–30.

a tradition among the Fathers of the Church, one that seems to go back to the Cappadocians of the fourth century, that goes in that direction. They see in the doctrine of the Trinity the simultaneous rejection of what they saw as two extremes, the Jewish position and the pagan. The idea of a Trinitarian god would be situated beyond the teeming number of battling gods, but also would go beyond the narrowness of a single God lacking the Word and the Spirit.[21] Here, however, one has to guard against a misunderstanding. Whatever is the meaning and value of this turning one's back on Judaism and paganism (in my view, it has precious little), in no case does it signify that the number three means more than one but less than the multitude of the pagan gods, as if the Trinity simply meant "not too much, not too little." It must be recognized that faith in the Trinity has nothing to do with belief in three gods. This heresy was formally condemned under the name of "tritheism." To be sure, one can ask if any Christian thinker ever espoused it, whether it simply might be a category in a formal list of erroneous opinions. On the other hand, it is often the idea of the Trinity that its adversaries have, sometimes because of the inaccurate presentations of the doctrine offered by Christians themselves.

Before we turn to the Trinitarian dimensions, let us return to another affirmation. Christianity certainly confesses one God. A sole God "who neither engenders nor was engendered," a formula that is not at all the sole property of Islam (*Quran*, CXII, 3), but which is rooted in the philosophers before Socrates, is continued in neoplatonism, and emerges at the beginning of the thirteen century as the official teaching of the Catholic faith.[22] As a result, do

21 Cf. Gregory of Nyssa, *Discours catéchétique*, III, 203, ed. L. Méridier (Paris, Picard, 1908), pp. 18–20. The idea is found in Maximus the Confessor and John Damascene.

22 See Philolaos, DK 44 B 20, in H. Diels and W. Kranz, *Die Fragmente der Vorsokratiker* (Dublin and Berlin, Weidmann, 1952), t. 1, p. 426; then Macrobius, *Commentaire sur le Songe de Scipion*, I, 5, 16; ed. J. Willis (Stuttgart, Teubner, 1963), p. 17, 31; Candid the Arian, *Lettre à Marius Victorinus*, 1, in *Oeuvres Théologiques*, ed. P. Hadot, *Sources Chrétiennes*, n. 68 (Paris, Le Cerf, 1960), p. 106;

we have to place Christianity in the camp of monotheism, with it being a simple variant? Here we have to take certain precautions. And to do this, pose the question properly.

2. *Uniqueness and unity*

We distinguish uniqueness and unity. To be unique and to be one do not mean the same thing. To say that God is unique means that there is but one God, that there is not a plurality of gods. In contrast, to say that God is one means to say that God is simple, that there is no plurality in God. These two senses of "oneness" are not necessarily connected. Nothing forbids imagining that there is one God but who is composed; or conversely, that there are several gods, each of which is simple. If one applies this distinction, one sees that, strictly speaking, "monotheism" only attributes one of these meanings to God, i.e., uniqueness: of the gods, there is but one example. From this point of view, it appears that one has a simple response to the problem posed by the doctrine of the Trinity. It would consist in saying that there exists one God in three persons, but this occurs in only one instance. Christians, therefore, do not have more gods than others.

This solution, however, is as unhelpful as the concept of monotheism which inevitably suggests it. The religions that have proclaimed that God is one have never contented themselves with only saying that he was the only one. They also said that he was "without division." This is what Islam says, taking the common interpretation of the rather obscure expression (*al-samad*) found in the sura entitled "pure worship" (*al-ikhlâs*), n. CXII. In truth, the question of the uniqueness of God is too abstract a question, as long as it is separated from the question of his unity. And the two ideas that we have distinguished rather rigorously were not set in opposition in the ancient world, when paganism and

finally, the IV Lateran Council (1215), in H. Denzinger and C. Bannwart, *Enchiridion symbolorum definitionum et declarationum de rebus fidei et morum* (Fribourg, Herder, 1908, #432 (358)), p. 191.

Judaism, then Christianity, encountered one another, and the latter sought to formulate its faith.[23] This inseparability proved to be very fruitful, more than the scalpel of logic would have been.

3. The concrete problem

Let us therefore try to sketch, at least in broad strokes, the concrete backdrop of the problem. One point was never, or hardly ever, called into question: there is something divine in the universe. This vague affirmation, almost a simple observation, does not assume that "the divine" (grammatically neutral) necessarily takes a personal aspect. When Aristotle seeks to summarize the truth-content of the myths, he reduces it to the proposition according to which "the divine" (to theion) encompasses (periechei) the order of nature."[24] And Epicurus's gods, even if they are a bit vague, by their presence in the "interworlds," constitute a sort of connective tissue.

A second point also went more or less without saying: the divine is bound to itself and forms something like a world (whether mythological or cosmological), a sphere of existence with its own laws, which connects those who participate in the divine nature with one another. Homer says that beautifully in two verses, when he explains how Hermes could identify Calypso, even though he has never seen her: "The gods are not unknown to each other, even if they live far apart."[25] The divine substance is one, in the sense that everything that is divine possesses identical characteristics. This unity is that of a genus, or of matter.

The concrete alternative of monotheism or polytheism appears against this backdrop of the divine substance. And the question that each, and both, respond to, insofar as we can reconstitute it, was therefore not so much the number of gods than of the *concentration of the divine:* what *is* divine in the universe, what has the right to the title of god, of divine substance? Or if one wishes, can

23 See Ch. Stead, *Divine Substance* (Oxford, Clarendon Press, 1977), pp. 181–83.
24 Aristotle, *Metaphysics*, XII, 8, 1074b3.
25 Homer, *Odyssey*, 5, 79–80.

it crystallize in several points or does it have to congeal in a single possessor? This is the way that the philosopher Numenius of Apamea (second century C.E.) posed the problem: "The First God, who abides in himself, is simple (*haplous*) from the fact that entirely concentrated in himself (*heautôi suggignomenos diolou*), he cannot be divided."[26] In the following century, Plotinus posed it in the same terms and pronounced himself against such a concentration of the divine: "It is not to concentrate (*susteilai*) [the divine] in a single thing, but to show that it is several, as it itself showed, this is the view of men who know the power of God." This was a passage that Nietzsche will cite almost literally several centuries later.[27]

Historically speaking, it appears that one sees the birth of monotheism when a god supplants the others to the point of eliminating them. Even the God of Israel distinguishes himself from the background of a court of gods (*Psalm* 82, 1). In this perspective, unity and uniqueness coincide: the concentration or the diffusion of the divine substance either forbids or allows the plurality of gods. Where the concentration of the divine is at its highest degree of compression, there God is absolutely one (= simple), there can only be one God, who is also absolutely one (= unique). The problem of monotheism versus polytheism thus bears less upon God than upon the divine. To insist upon the absolute simplicity of the divine would be therefore a sufficient means of excluding the plurality of the gods of paganism.

Is it necessary, therefore, to think that Christianity, as it were, has given the divine substance enough "flexibility" that it can admit of three persons? And that in this way it stops part-way on the road that, since the prophets, leads to the affirmation of the absolute simplicity of God? The case is quite the opposite: Christianity goes to the very end of this way; it even, perhaps, goes beyond. In truth, the question is not *whether* God is one

26 Numenius, *Fragments*, n. 11, ed. E. des Places (Paris, les Belles Lettres, 1973), p. 53.
27 Plotinus, *Enneads*, II, 9 [33], 9, 35–37; Nietzsche, *Also sprach Zarathustra*, III, 8, KSA, t. 4, p. 431.

(something that is acquired doctrine concerning him, going almost without saying), but *how* he is one.

It does not appear that this question was posed outside of Christianity, when people were content to say that the unity of God is such that it has nothing in common with the different ways that things in the created world can be one. In saying this, no one said how we can *understand* what is said when we hear that "God is one" (*Deuteronomy*, 6, 4). Even if, when God is compared to a creature, resemblance is always more than compensated by dissimilarity, there still has to remain a minimum of resemblance, so that what we say can have *some* intelligibility.[28] Without this, negation would lead to atheism. "Intelligible" however is only a provisional term; in this case above all others, it is important, not to understand, but to allow oneself to be understood. It would be better to say, "confessable," so that the unity of God can be confessed and not simply acknowledged, so that it can be the object of a gift of self on the part of the believer.

III. Union: the human model

1. The bond of charity

I will borrow the answer to the question of how God is one, not from a theologian, but from a "mystic" of the twelfth century, St. Bernard of Clairvaux. He affirms that the bond that maintains the unity of God is nothing other than charity.[29] His formulation is particularly clear, but it is rooted in a long tradition of reflection on the Holy Spirit as love and the internal bond of the Trinity. In its teaching on the Trinity, Christian dogmatics, even when it makes use of the most abstract instruments of logic in order to formulate with some precision what, at bottom, is finally

---

28 IV Lateran Council (1215), in Denzinger and Bannwart, *op. cit.*, #432 (358), p. 192.

29 Bernard of Clairvaux, *De l'amour de Dieu*, XII, 35, *Opera*, t. III, p. 149 (also: *Patrologia Latina*, 182, 996 AB).

inexpressible, does not say anything else. It even says something that seems to us perfectly paradoxical. The same St. Bernard who says that charity is the unity of the three persons also says that this unity is stronger and more "one" than all others.[30]

This affirmation hardly corresponds to our human experience of love; one could even say it is diametrically opposed. This is why we ought to begin by being astonished at the claim. In truth, we find it difficult to conceive how love can produce a unity that is something other than a *façon de parler*, a manner of speaking. Now, we know very well that love leads to a certain union: coupling brings together sexual partners and, in specifically human love, it leads to an even deeper common life, one that encompasses all the dimensions of the personality, making for a certain communion of souls. But the desire to be solely one with the beloved can only be satisfied in myth or metaphor. In this way, Aristophanes says that lovers desire that the divine artificer Hephaistos would solder them back together.[31] Nonetheless, it remains true that for the one who considers things soberly, the unity spoken about when it is said of two friends or two lovers that "they make only one" is the weakest of all the types of unity distinguished by philosophers.

This unity is purely relative, in the sense of the Aristotelian category of relation (*pros ti*).[32] It does not really change those it unites. If the one I love were to disappear, or I cease to love her, in a certain sense, nothing is changed in me. In contrast, at the other extreme of unity, if the unity of an object or a person with himself disappeared, the object itself, or the person himself, would disintegrate and disappear. We, therefore, are naturally inclined to consider the unity that assures the coherence of a being with itself as being tighter, more intimate, than that which links two beings with each other. As a consequence, the strong type of unity seems to be monotheism. And it is often this model of unity that we apply to

---

30 Idem., *De la considération*, V, III, 19, *Opera*, t. III, p. 483. Also see St. Augustine, *De la Trinité*, XV, xxiii, 43, BA, t. 16, p. 538.
31 Plato, *Symposium*, 192de.
32 Aristotle, *Categories*, 7.

God when we call ourselves "monotheists."[33] And if we profess faith in the Trinity, the diversity of persons emerges from the different points of view cast on the seamless unity of the godhead. From the perspective of orthodox theology, however, this means that we have fallen into the heresy we mentioned earlier, "modalism."

2. Love and identity

At this point, though, we have to acknowledge that the sovereign type of unity we just discussed does not count much vis-à-vis the experience of unity we have in love. And while we might recognize that it is the most "superficial" of all the ways of being one, it is infinitely more valuable than the unshatterable unity of a diamond. If, in a certain way the disappearance of the beloved does not "do" anything to us, on another hand, it does everything. And, against all logic, who would not choose the latter? There is something in us that would prefer only to exist by loving, even to the point of dying with the one we love, or for him, as Alcestis did in the tragedy of Euripides. And we curse the burdensome limits of our nature. We all know that the unity that binds us to the beloved counts more that our mere identity with ourselves. That is why we desire for our love to transform us, to the point of rendering us unrecognizable, to the point of losing our identity. Nothing would bring us more joy that to hear said of us, what is said of lovers: "I no longer recognize him!"

Love, therefore, is for us both the most important and the least, the most central and the most peripheral, of the types of unity. The highest unity and the strongest unity are two different things. The most exquisite aspect of our existence, its highest summit, is also the most fragile. This is why human love is always accompanied by a certain melancholy. One can generalize and extend to all the dimensions of love what a libertine in Laclos's *Dangerous Liaisons* said of coitus: "We're always two."[34] If love

33 A. de Saint-Exupéry, *Citadelle*, LXXIII, ed. R. Caillois (Paris, Gallimard, "Bibliothèque de la Pléiade," 1959), p. 683.
34 C. de Laclos, *Les Liaisons dangereuses*, Letter 5.

only results in a relatively feeble union, this is because it connects two terms that are external to one another, and who are first of all not defined by this connection but by much more essential characteristics, such as sex, age, language, profession, character. I am myself, before being the husband of my wife, the father of my children, the friend of my friends.

However, what appears to be a source of melancholy does not only have negative aspects. For us, the fusion of beings that we dream of could not occur except by a sort of ingestion, the assimilation of the other to ourselves. The praying mantis has human equivalents, and not only among "the female of the species," although, as Kipling said, she is deemed to be" more deadly than the male."[35] On the other hand, love worthy of the name begins with respect for the other in his or her difference, and continues with the acknowledgement that each is irreducible to what connects him with the other (to be merely "the wife of John" (the title of a French film) is not very flattering . . . . Eventually it is crowned with the sacrifice that prefers the other to oneself. In this case, one will be tempted to apply this model to God and to represent the Trinity as a sort of triumvirate, a confederation of three gods bound by intense affection. Such an image (called "tritheist") would appear to allow us to acknowledge the love present in God. But it is no less false than the previous image (called "modalist"). It, too, naively transposes a human experience to God. To be sure, it is truly a genuine experience of love. But to apply it to God is to blind oneself to the fact that what allows love to exist in us is also what radically limits it.

3. To accept the other as another

Let us, therefore, look more closely. Love, I said, must respect the irreducible alterity of the beloved. Simone Weil gave it a magnificent formulation: "To love purely is to consent to distance, it is even to adore the distance between oneself and what one loves."[36]

35 R. Kipling, *The Female of the Species* (1911).
36 S. Weil, *La Pesanteur et la Grâce* [1947] (Paris, UGE, 1962), p. 71.

But whence comes this otherness? It is even exterior to the beloved. It has nothing to do with love given or returned. It is given even before the birth of love. It comes in fact from the natural diversity of individuals. I am other because I am defined by a certain number of characteristics that I received from my parents, my education, my past history. Respect for difference, a respect that constitutes love, always comes after the fact. It cannot but model itself on the natural diversity that it does not produce but finds already existing. As a consequence, the wonderfulness of singularity is always threatened with turning into the contingency of the natural, like wine into vinegar. This is what happens when love grows cold. Think of domestic scenes. The marvel of singularity is reduced to a brute fact. "That's just how you are!" Worse, the liberty of the person seems to be undermined by the necessities of nature: "Just like your mother!" Even in the times when everything seems fine, the enthusiastic acceptance of the other as a free person always remains in the path that *can* lead to the resigned acceptance of "matter of fact."

Human love can only *accept*, more or less well, the otherness of what it loves. But it cannot *produce* this alterity. As a result, it goes both too far and not far enough in union, and in alterity. Not far enough in union, because it fails to produce a single being out of the two; it is tempted to go too far, though, because it could only produce this union by devouring the other. At the same time, it goes too far in alterity because the persons remain exterior to one another; while it does not go far enough, because their distinction is only ratified, not chosen.

If someone asks why this is the case, I would give a double answer, in the two registers of finitude and of sin. We are finite beings because we are divided beings, in each of us there are two aspects. I am a personal, singular, irreplaceable being, but there is also in me a "natural" dimension, taken in a large sense to encompass everything I have received. What in love unites us to the beloved being is the result of what we have that is most personal and most free. In saying this, I am not unaware of the attempts in the human sciences to connect love as such to what belongs to us naturally (again, in a large sense including the sub-conscious or social programming). I believe, however, that I can disregard them, because rather than explaining love they destroy it. They do so precisely by the fact that they attempt to explain it. A love that is explained is not love, or it is an illusory love.

If love is personal and free, or it does not exist, it remains true that what we give the beloved is freighted with a nature. And the same is true of what we love in the other. That is why, as we have seen, that love remains imperfect on both the plane of otherness and of union. With respect to the first, it cannot but respond to an already given difference at the biological, social, or cultural level. As for the second, union risks being nothing but a fusion because it is to us and our nature that love assimilates the beloved. The beloved will imitate our character and submit to our habits. What our finitude makes possible, sin renders real. What is personal in us sins by rejecting living out of personal liberty and by seeking to possess what in us is natural. Only liberty sins, but it sins by preferring to itself what allows itself to be possessed. Hence, union becomes the process of causing the other to lose her nature for the sake of ours.

In a word, human love is limited, which allows it to be sinful, that is, to change into its opposite. It is this way, because what connects us to the beloved does not exhaust what we are. The relation that ties us to the other is not the same thing as our nature. In other words, love is something we experience, that we live, that we possess – however one would like to put it. But it is never by itself what we *are*.

IV. Union: the Trinitarian model

It is precisely here that the novelty of the Christian conception of love appears, such that it explains why Christians confess a Trinitarian God. It is contained in a single phrase of the New Testament: "God is love" (I *John*, 4, 16).

1. Relation

I will not encumber myself with exegetical niceties. I will take the phrase literally, giving the verb "is" its fullest sense, as if one meant to say: what God is, is love, and nothing else. A love that is not, as in our case, something we "have," but what God is. A love, therefore, that is wholly freed from the limitations imposed upon us by the fact that it is the property of a nature that does not coincide with it. To repeat: the doctrine of the Trinity is nothing else than the stubborn effort to get to the bottom of this sentence of St. John. Everything said of the three Persons or of the three hypostases in the divine substance that the Christian churches confess is rooted in the logic of charity. It thus is the promotion – undreamt of by the philosophers – of the concept of relation. They only saw in relation "an offshoot of being," a category used to denote merely what is most marginal to substance.[37] In Christian theology it is promoted to the status of the key that allows one to think what God truly is. The dogma of the Trinity maintains that the three divine Persons are not distinguished in anything (they have, or are, the same substance), except for the relations that unite them. To be a father is not the same thing as to be a son, even if there can't be a father without a son, or a son without a father. To be the Father is not to be the Son, but "to have" the Son, that is, to engender the Son. To illustrate, let us use a rule formulated by St. Augustine, one that initially appears to be wholly abstract. What is said of one of the persons and which only applies to that person is said "relatively" of the others.[38] Here logic is trying to follow charity as closely as it can, to the point that the meaning of the concept permits itself to be translated into the logic of gift: what each person possesses is only possessed by giving it to another! Each person *is* the relation it "has" with the others. St. Thomas expresses this with his concept of "subsisting relation."[39]

37 Aristotle, *Nicomachean Ethics*, I, 6, 1096a21.
38 St. Augustine, *De la Trinité*, V, xi, 12, BA, t. 15, p. 450 (see also VI, ii, 3, *ibid.*, p. 472).
39 St. Thomas, *Summa theologiae*, I, q. 29, a. 4.

This relation, however, is nothing else but love. A theologian of the twelfth century, Richard of Saint-Victor, was able to push the logic of love further along. In his treatise on Trinitarian theology, he ventured something of a deduction of the Trinity from charity. Charity, he said, is only possible when there are two persons. And it finds its perfection when each of the two wills that the beloved be loved by a third person. In so doing, Richard did not transpose into God something like the human family. On the contrary, he liberated love from what limits it in man and among men, since in God alone are being and loving identical. Thus, it is the case that "for each of the three, the person and his love are one and the same thing. To be several persons in a single divinity is nothing other than the fact of having one and the same supreme love, or rather of being this same love, which nonetheless is a different property in each. In God, a person is nothing other than this supreme love, which in each case is distinguished by a definite property. . . . Each person is the same thing as his love."[40]

In this way, the duality between what is natural and what is personal does not exist in God. In the Trinity, each person is characterized by the relation that is proper to him. And, if this relation is defined vis-à-vis the other persons who are the terms (*termini*) of the relation, the relation itself is nothing other than God himself.[41]

2. To give rise to the other

In God, the relation that distinguishes each person is precisely what unites him to the others. The divine love does not know the limits of our love. This can be seen on two important points.

On one hand, this can be seen in what concerns the rapport to the other. For us, the difficulty of love consists in accepting the other as different from us, for God, or rather in God, the other is not someone that one has to resign oneself to accepting. In God, love does much more: it gives rise to the other, when the Father

40 Richard of St.-Victor, *La Trinité*, V, 20, ed. G. Salet, *Sources chrétiennes*, n. 63 bis (Paris, Le Cerf, 1959), p. 352.
41 St. Thomas, *Summa theologiae*, I, q. 28, a. 2.

engenders the Son, and when both produce (in technical terms: "spirate") the Spirit. And love *is* this posing, or giving rise to, the other as other. The Father is not Father except by engendering the Son. Posing the other as such communicates the divine substance to the other. The other is thus not possessed, but given. Or one could say that it is not possessed except as given. It certainly is not a "deity" that exists outside the relationship, outside the activity of the charity that gives itself. It does not exist outside the gift that is constituted by love and which is love.

On the other hand, this can be seen in what concerns the unifying role of love. In God love does not attach external terms or subjects to one another. It unites God to himself, by constituting his very unity. Thus, what is separated in us co-incides in God. In him, the highest union is also the strongest. This unity is love, a love that is nothing but the fact of posing otherness. Thus love brings it about that the Father and the Son are one, not in the sense that it prevents the Son from being another, but because it gives him "other-being," and that the Father himself is nothing but this giving.

Now one can better understand the meaning of the doctrine that the theologians designate by the technical term of the "monarchy" (*monos-arche*) of the Father. According to this teaching, the Father is the sole person of the Trinity who does not have a principle (*arche*), while the Son has the Father for principle, and the Spirit has the Father and the Son united in one as its principle. This doctrine does not attribute some privileged independence to the Father. The Father cannot be the Father without the Son, since without the Son would he still be Father? To say that the Father does not have a principle is to say that he is a principle, nothing more. One can venture the following formulation: he is his own source in order to be able, on his own, to engender the Son. To speak in this way is to say that he engages himself entirely, and with full liberty, in the gift by which he engenders the Son. By engendering him, he is what he is, to wit: the Father. The "monarchy" of the Father thus results, if I can use this term in referring to what is eternal, from a process. God is one because he is united. Here we can cite Hegel: "In the true Trinity, what is achieved is not simply unity but also accord

(*Einigkeit*), the conclusion (*Schluss*) which results in a unity *full of content* and wholly *effective*, a unity which in its wholly concrete determination is the Spirit."[42]

Thus, what in Christianity corresponds – if one wishes to make this connection – to what could receive elsewhere the name of monotheism is the doctrine of the Trinity. This doctrine is not a corrective made after the fact, a little water added to the pure wine of divine unity. Nor is it a relaxing of the monotheistic idea. On the contrary, it is an explication of this idea. It deepens the confession of the *fact* that God is one, by means of the *manner* in which He is one. *The Trinity is the manner in which God is one.* This manner is charity. "God is so essentially love that the unity which, in a sense, is his definition, is a simple effect of love."[43] And it is because this unity is a unity of charity that it is Trinitarian. The interior life of the Trinity, which simultaneously unites and distinguishes, has no other law in God but itself, it is the free play of this law that makes God the Trinity. For Christians, to say that "God is one" is a way of saying that "God is love." In the same way, all the other names they give to God are but different ways of coining the gold of charity.

Conclusion: united to the one God?

Assuming that the Trinitarian doctrine conveys something of the mystery of God's unity, this should not become a platform for for us to go about discoursing at even greater length about him and thus satisfying our curiosity. It is exactly the opposite. This curiosity is excluded by the very fact that God is love. Where the object that one wants to know is love, the desire simply to know would be pure voyeurism. The voyeur who remains outside of love in fact

42 G. W. F. Hegel, *Wissenschaft der Logik*, ed. G. Lasson (Hambourg, Meiner, 1967), t. 1, p. 338.
43 S. Weil, "L'amour de Dieu et le malheur" (1942), in *Oeuvres*, ed. F. de Lussy (Paris, Gallimard, 1999), p. 698.

understands nothing, because love does not invite us merely to know it, but to share it. And it is precisely for this that the mystery was revealed to us. The way in which God is one is not without implications for the way in which we have to conduct ourselves. And "implications" is too weak; "imperatives" is better. These include how we relate to this divine unity, then how we conduct ourselves in the world, toward everything that is either one or multiple.

Vis-à-vis the unity of God, the Trinitarian nature of God invites us to adopt a distinctive attitude. If the unity of God were a simple fact (even if this fact were revealed), we could only acknowledge it. If to this fact is added its reason, if we understand *why* God is one, we can give our faith a more precise content. But we would continue to have, vis-à-vis this content, the attitude of one who merely acknowledges and notes that. . . . In contrast, we cannot, properly speaking, *confess* the unity of God except if we are given the way in which God is one, i.e., in charity, in which the fact and the reason are identical. If I love, I have no other reason for loving than the fact that I love, and this fact is sufficient unto itself. If God is love, we understand why he is one. But we understand *in the way that love is understood*, by understanding that we cannot merely understand it. "Cannot understand" here is completely different from a counsel of despair. On the contrary, it is an appeal to allow oneself to be understood, to enter into what presents itself to be understood. No one understands love except by loving. The unity of God is worthy of being loved because it is love. To confess this unity, therefore, is to love it. It is given to us to do so in the Holy Spirit, the bond of divine unity. The confession of divine unity is in fact what is proper to the Spirit. It is by giving us the Holy Spirit – his own bond of unity – that God give us the power to confess this unity.

To confess the unity of God is, as such, to be united to him. But with a unity that is analogous to his. God is freely united to himself. To be united to God is therefore to unite one's liberty to God's freedom. Two freedoms cannot unite as do material objects, by means of fusion or agglomeration. The highest union is the union of wills, in which there is not a mixture but accord, a union that, far from dissolving the identity of each its terms, enhances it.

Chapter 4
God the Father

As we just saw, the God of Christians is a Trinity: Father, Son, and Holy Spirit. In this chapter, I would like to bring some additional clarity to the first of these three terms. In has the special interest of corresponding to a fundamental human experience, that of procreation. This is a trait it shares with the second term ("Son"), which is unthinkable without it, because one is always a father of a child and the child of a father. This is a trait that also distinguishes it from the third term, the "Holy Spirit," which does not directly correspond to a human experience. What paternity and filiation are, each person has some idea; many men are fathers and all, without exception, had a father. To be sure, the theologians put us on guard: this correspondence is only an analogy. It does not allow us – not without a thousand precautions – simply to rise from what the human meaning of the term "father" means to God.

Here, however, I would like to take the word "Father" as designating a certain mode of the relationship of God to creation, and to human beings in particular. I place myself therefore on a lower level than that of the Trinity, which concerns what God is in himself (in technical terminology: "theology"), in order to examine what the relation is between God and what is not-God ("economy").

1. Sexuality and the image of God

Procreation, which makes certain men fathers and all children, is rooted in sexuality. Now, Christians, like the Jews before them, have said about sexuality something that derives directly from

}69{

their way of conceiving God. For them, the relationship between the sexes is supposed to contain the trace, or be one of the traces, of the creation of human being by God. From the beginning, the Bible tells us that God created man in his image, and it immediately adds: "Male and female He created them." (*Genesis*, 1, 27). In making man in his image, God made him male and female.

We first should observe that this view of sexual division understands it to be a positive thing. This is not at all self-evident, it does not go without saying. The fact that each of us is male or female, but never the two, is the sign that we are finite beings, incapable of forming a complete whole. One can see in this a negative fact, a kind of condemnation. The myth of Aristophanes in Plato's Symposium explains the sexual division by an operation of Zeus that cut in half primitive spheres that were either bisexual or entirely male or female.[1]

Next, if it is *as sexual* that man is the image of God, then there ought to be something in God that resembles sexuality. Let me try to specify what is new here. That a God has some relationship with sexuality is not extraordinary. It is even banal. Religions often represent their gods as sexual, even as more sexual than mortals. This was especially the case with the civilizations that surrounded ancient Israel, on the basis of which Israel had to define its own religion. In these religions, which later were called "pagan," the gods were charged, above all, with assuring, by means of rain, the abundance of the harvest, and guaranteeing that the flocks reproduced abundantly. Therefore, whether they took on the form of a human being or an animal, the deity had to display signs of exuberant fecundity. One therefore encounters everywhere Venuses with teeming breasts andd male gods with permanent erections.

But if the God of Israel created in his own image a being who is male and female, does that mean that he contains the two sexes, that he is bisexual? Or, perhaps, that he is above the two sexes and thus asexual? If this were the case, it would not be particularly

---

1   Plato, *Symposium*, 189d–193c.

remarkable: the myths presented androgynous gods, such as Hermaphrodite, a proper name become an adjective.

However, nothing allows us to suppose that the God of Israel is bisexual or asexual, that he is either beyond the sexual difference or above sexuality in general. Quite the contrary. The name of YHWH, grammatically speaking, is masculine. And, in their great majority, biblical images also imply a masculine figure. For example, the God of Israel is the male spouse of his people. The prophet Hosea used an image from his own life for this purpose. There are exceptions, let us recount a few. YHWH is compared to a mother who consoles her children in Isaiah (66, 13). The same is true of God's Spirit. In semitic languages, metereological phenomena are often enough given a feminine name. This is true of wind, and with it "spirit," which is designated by the same term. When "Spirit" is a divine name, the word is therefore feminine. These facts are well known, sometimes overemphasized. It remains true, though, that the dominant biblical image is of a masculine God. Should we see in it the heavenly projection of a patriarchal society, one dominated by males? A projection that would provide transcendent legitimacy to it, hence the means to perpetuate itself in minds as well as in social reality?

We need to look closer at the masculinity of the God of Israel. To begin with, YHWH does not have a divine spouse, as does Zeus (Hera), and even less does he have adventures with mortal women. Nor is there a "paredre," a little female partner, as do the semitic gods of the west. This is true at least among the elites of Israel. The common run were less strict. Papyri discovered in upper Egypt from the Jewish military colony stationed in Elephantine by the Persians in the fifth century before Christ seem to have worshiped, alongside YHWH, a female deity called 'Anathbethel.[2] But the normative religion of Israel, as found in the

2   See A. E. Cowley, *Aramaic Papyri of the Fifth Century B.C.* (Oxford, Clarendon Press, 1923) Papyrus n. 22 [Names of the Contributors to Temple Funds], col. IV, I. 123–25, p. 70; trad. P. 72; commentary p. 76; see also the Introduction, pp. XVIII-XIX.

writings of the Old Testament, did not associate any female partner with its God.

2. Masculinity and virility

From this, one can draw an important consequence in the form of a distinction between masculinity and virility. Modern French means above all by "virility" sexual potency, the capacity of a male to impregnate a female. Virility is the ability to fulfill the function of a spouse; in Latin, *vir*. Now, the masculinity of the God of Israel is not virility, as we just saw, it is not oriented toward a divine female figure.

In this way, the sexual relation is not found within the world of the divine. It finds itself free to engage in another domain. As a result, it can exercise itself between God and his people. This is why the prophets portray God as the spouse of Israel, a promiscuous woman who betrays him with others. They play upon the word *ba'al*, which means "husband," but which is also the name of the gods of the Canaanites. Hence, too, the "domestic scenes" in which the recollection of the honeymoon is joined with threats of repudi-ation, themselves trumped by the immutable fidelity of God, always followed by promises of reconciliation. This powerfully developed nuptial image gave rise to the allegorical interpretation of the *Song of Songs*, which in turn allowed Rabbi Akiba to have this song of love, originally of profane meaning, accepted into the canon of Scripture.[3] It led to ideas of "mystical marriage" which have contin-ued in Christianity as well as kabbalistic and Hassidic Judaism until our days. In any case, it implies that it is the relationship between God and humanity that is called to enter into the divine sphere itself. One can even see in it a prefiguration of the Incarnation.

Sexuality, therefore, teaches us something about the relation-ship of God to man, but not specifically about God's nature. What is the deepest foundation of this relationship? The relationship of

3   Rabbi Aquiba in *Mishnah*, the treatise *Yadayim*, III, 5, English trans-lation in, *The Mishnah*, H. Danby (Oxford, Oxford University Press, 1933), p. 782.

God to the people of Israel is an alliance, a covenant. By this very fact, it is viewed through the images of the conjugal bond. There is more, however. From the beginning of the reflections of Israel on its experience of God, and more and more clearly as it proceeds, the choice of his people by God is understood to be that which constitutes the people as a people. It was not a preexisting people that God chose for himself; quite the contrary: God chose a people for himself (*Deut.*, 4, 34). Thus it is the covenant with God that constitutes the people. The divine initiative is total. In this way, one advances to the idea of the absolute initiative of God, preceded by nothing. This idea is the idea of creation.

3. Creation and paternity

The affirmation according to which man – man as sexual, as man-and-woman – is the image of God, this affirmation is located in an account of creation. We are men and women because we are in the image of God. But we are men-and-women-in-the-image-of-God because we are created. It is the context of creation that illumines everything. Creation reveals God to us as radically taking the initiative, by means of an act preceded by nothing, thus conditioned by nothing, and hence totally free. In this way, the creative act takes to its conclusion the logic of the initiative of divine election. God was as free to create as he was to choose – and even to constitute – a people.

The idea of creation, applied first of all implicitly to the people, then explicitly to the entirety of what exists, entails another image, one that is added to the conjugal image of YHWH as the spouse of Israel. The biblical God appears as the father of his people, who is his son (*Hosea,* 11, 1), his eldest son (*Exodus,* 4, 22). This image is not self-evident. To be sure, it has prefigurations in other religions, but is only fully developed in Judaism and Christianity. In contrast, one can note the following capital fact: the God of Islam is not called "father," and Muslim piety does not place this term among the ninety-nine "most beautiful names of God" listed in the tradition.

Because he creates, God reveals himself as father. But the idea of creation, in turn, brings a decisive correction to the idea of paternity. In a word: *the idea of paternity is severed from the idea of virility*. In the biological domain, a father is first of all a male. He becomes a father by his capacity to impregnate a women whom he makes a mother. He cannot be a father by himself (except in the Egyptian myth, in which the original god produced the world by masturbation[4]). In reality, though, there has to be some "favorable soil." The initiative of God, however, is so total that he has no need of anyone. St. Gregory of Nyssa could venture a bold phrase and speak of God's "virginal fatherhood."[5]

In other words, God is father but not male. And it is not sufficient to say that he is father *even though* he is not male. One has to go further and risk the formula that, if he can be father, the absolute Father, it is precisely because he is not male. This sundering paternity from virility is exactly what the Quran fails to do. It understands fatherhood on the model of our human experience, and even on the model of the broader phenomenon of begetting, that is to be seen among the largest number of living beings. Now, if one accepts this premise, the consequence rigorously follows: God could not be father unless he had a sexual partner; which is not the case; hence he is not a father. And in particular, Jesus can't possibly be the son of God. In this way, the Sura *The Cattle* asks, in a question which is obviously rhetorical in nature : "How could He have a child, since He has no mate" *(sāhiba)*[6]

A certain asymmetry appears at this point. God is father, even absolute Father, but he is not mother. In order to understand this, let us reflect for a moment on what distinguishes paternity from maternity at the level of our human experience. The mother draws the child growing within her from her own flesh. To be sure, the

4   See the two versions in E. A. Wallis Budge, *Legends of the Egyptian Gods. Hieroglyphic Texts and Translations* (New York, Dover, 1994 [1912]), pp. 4–5 & 10–11.

5   Gregory of Nyssa, *On virginity*, 2; *PG*, 46, 321c. Quoted in L. Bouyer, *Le Trône de la Sagesse. Essai sur la signification du culte marial* (Paris, Cerf, 1961), p. 147.

6   *Quran*, VI, n° 55, v. 101.

father contributes a bit of his flesh, but only in the limited instant of fertilization. This does not lead to the co-belonging of the infant and his progenitor. The child never is part of the body of his father. In contrast, during the period of gestation the child is one with his mother, if not strictly biologically speaking, at least in the way in which the mother experiences him. Analogously, God creates something that is not consubstantial with him. "The mother, and more mythically, any female deity, has this fundamental difference from God: she remains with the child. The entire time. While the father, like God, in principle has already disappeared."[7]

To be sure, one can certainly represent creation, once it has come into being, as "contained" in God, as enveloped in his providential care. This sort of solicitude evokes maternal images. Moreover, one can observe that Christianity has given a central role to a woman, the Virgin Mary, who draws to herself all the activities belonging to femininity, above all, maternity. But this maternal activity toward creatures is itself the action of a creature that never was divinized. Conversely, the act of creation has never been held in Christianity to be the creation of something that is consubstantial with God.

What is at stake in the point is nothing less than a certain conception of liberty. A father has *to recognize* his child once he is born. Certain civilizations, Rome for example, have made a religious ritual of this necessity. But even when this was not the case, when nothing underscored the fact and made it explicit, the reality subsisted. The father recognized his child in an act of liberty that nothing could compel him to give. The mother on the other hand knows very well that the child is hers because he grew in her. She cannot not acknowledge the child as hers. Thus the child finds himself vis-à-vis his father in a relationship of liberty that cannot be his with his mother. We can illustrate this difference by means of the difference between "the fatherland" (*patrie*) and "the nation." A country of origin, understood as one's fatherland, can become the object of a patriotism that is elective. As the Latin

7   P. Muray, *Le XIXe siècle à travers les ages* (Paris, Denoël, 1984, rééd. "Tel," 1999), p. 445.

ON THE GOD OF THE CHRISTIANS

phrase puts it, *ubi bene, ibi patria* ("The fatherland is wherever one finds oneself well."). In contrast, where there is a common mother, the nation (in the etymological sense of *natio*, the progeny of a female animal), and the underlying sentiment which nourishes national-feeling, there is an unchosen bond.

4. *The uncoupling of paternity and virility*

Every image of God, be it a picture or a concept, has to be constantly critiqued by tracing it back to its ineffable original, and by playing off it other images that contradict it. It remains, though, that some images are better than others. In this context, all things being equal, the image of paternity for creation is preferable to that of maternity. But God's paternity is not virility, as we have seen. As a consequence, the superiority of paternity does not entail a primacy of virility over femininity. God is father rather than mother. But he is not more male than female. And the fact that God is a father does not confer any privilege upon those, among human beings, whose masculine sex makes them capable of being fathers.

As St. Paul says, it is from the paternity of God that all paternity, in heaven and on earth, derives its name (*Ephesians*, 3, 15). This, though, is an appeal to rethink human paternity in the light of divine paternity. This entails purifying human paternity as much as possible from every element of "virility." This opens an immense horizon and program: highlighting free choice where there was only biological connection. To speak like St. Paul or St. Irenaeus, it is a matter of "recapitulating" everything in the register of freedom.[8] One would therefore extricate oneself from many impasses. Let us try to indicate a few.

From this, one can draw a certain attitude toward feminism. This is a legitimate movement. But one has to refuse to grant it any value over and above what is just. (This just-value will vary, depending upon the different tendencies and claims that can be

---

8 *Ephesians*, 1, 10; St. Irenaeus, *Contre les hérésies*, III, 21, 10, ed. F. Sagnard (Paris, Le Cerf, 1952), pp. 370–72, etc.

found within this nebulous movement and those who affiliate themselves with it.) But Christians as such do not have anything specifically Christian to say, beyond what philosophers, psychologists, sociologists, and other disciplines can offer. Christians need to underscore that the question does not have any immediate theological determination. What they know or believe they know about God does not *ipso facto* entitle them to intervene in the debates swirling around it, nor directly provide them with arguments for or against a particular position. For example, since it is severed from virility, the paternity of God cannot serve as a ground for any privilege for the masculine sex.

In other words, we need to distinguish the social domain from the theological. To falsely affirm that God is male can have grave social consequences. This false image can legitimate injustices, including the domestic tyranny of patriarchy. On the other hand, more accurate thought can help obtain greater justice in society. But, on the theological plane, to say that God is male is not worse than attributing to him any number of other inadequate attributes, or worse than saying that he is female. (It's not better, either.) For Christians, rejecting the "masculine" model of God is not essentially different from rejecting other false images. It is one case in the general theological operation of the "negative way," of criticizing any naïve application of human determinations to God.

Perhaps the most important consequence is to challenge a certain way in which we tend to conceive God's initiative. One cannot uncritically apply to God traits and features that derive from the conjugal life of men. Now, these relations are often conceived as a division of roles. To the male goes "initiative," while the female is characterized by "receptivity." One can think what one will about this division. It has the difficulty of mixing the natural and the social, and thus involving us in the chicken-or-the-egg problem.

It would be better, therefore, to simply reject the division based upon this image. The paternal initiative is not of the same order as that of virility, and thus God's initiative as creator who constitutes a people is not the same that belongs to the male in the sexual order, whether in constituting a family or educating his children. The latter initiative is a way of directing preexisting reality. But this is not God's relationship to what he creates. In this case, initiative is a gift made to the recipient, who receives not simply something that adds to what already exists, but his own existence and with it, the very capacity to receive.

This change of model has consequences for the political order. An initiative that would come from a merely-virile male (*sit venia verbo*) would simply be an initiative of power. A community that adopted it for its model would be founded solely upon a model of command. The model of authority in the Church, however, has always been conceived not as power, but as gift and service. Where the model of initiative is that of paternity rather than virility, it can only be construed as service. Christ's explicit words say as much: "Let the one who is greatest among you conduct himself as the least and he who commands, like one who serves" (*Luke*, 22, 26).

Conclusion

One cannot correctly understand how the sexual nature of man expresses his being the image of God without reference to the idea of creation. This idea entails a neutralization of the difference between the sexes, "neutralization," I say, not suppression, it is rendered not-relevant. In particular, it entails that virility has no privilege over femininity, neither in itself nor as an analogy of the divine. In contrast, paternity does possess advantages over maternity, but only when it is a question of deciding whether an image is more or less adequate to express the relationship of the creator to his work, not when it is a matter of comparing human activities. In Christianity, the sole task that awaits the virile male (in the sense we have given virility) is to imitate as well as possible the model of paternity (whether of the flesh or spirit), and to allow oneself to be more and more conformed to the God in whose image we all, male and female, have been created.

Chapter 5
A God Who Has Said Everything

As creator, the God of Christians, like the God of Judaism and of Islam, is a God who communicates with his creation. When this creature is man, a speaking being, this communication becomes speech. God speaks, or in any case, spoke. How does this word address itself to man insofar as he is human? And how can the power of a divine word allow man to exercise the liberty that makes him what he is?

I. Nothing more to say

1. Power, or the word

The power of a word ought to be at its height when the said word is authoritative, when it is a commanding word. It is nowhere more powerful than when it comes from those the Greeks, quite simply, called "the more powerful [than us]" (*hoi kreittones*), in other words, the gods. This is even more true when one is speaking about the one called "the All-Powerful." The most powerful word would be the divine word. Its power owes to its origin's divinity.

However, is the power of the divine word something we still can actually experience? Can we still experience a word of this sort? Does it not, rather, belong to a definitively passed period, and does not the fact that one evokes it today indicate a certain nostalgia, perhaps even a reactionary attitude? Does not speech today show us a much different face? That, for example of open discussion, which takes place within our democratic societies?

The first condition for that speech is the rejection of any authority that would claim to emanate from somewhere outside this democratic space. Now, this space is homogenous, unmarked by any sort of rank. The power of the speech that appears in it is that of arguments, and not of the source from whence they come. To be sure, it can happen that a word said to be "divine" enters the space, but then it cannot appeal to its divine source and has to convince by its content, and by that alone.

There is more. At the core of the spoken word, there is the *logos* ("reason," among other meanings) that it expresses. The power exercised by this *logos* is but one aspect of the entire word, what has been called "the power of the rational" (D. Janicaud).[1] This involves the capacity of the formula to arrange and to summon. In this way, the *logos* is powerful only as technical rationality, not as a living word addressed to a particular audience.

Thus, the time in which we live is really one of the radical impotence of speech. This sort of technical power and real speech mutually exclude one another. Where there is the power of technical mastery, which dictates and orders – because it previously has rendered everything quantifiable and countable – what wields power is no longer real speech. And wherever there is real speech in the democratic dialogue, power is excluded from the outset. Any given argument receives its power from the way in which it is received and accepted, not from the way in which it was uttered. Any discourse that claims authority because of its origin is, as such, deeply suspect, soon to be disqualified. This means that the divine word, precisely as divine, has no place in the modern world.

In fact, the modern world can be characterized as the time of the silence of the gods, or God. The long process of several centuries during which the world "modernized" no longer leaves room for divine words. The passage to modernity has been given several descriptions. Concerning the relationship of man to

---

1   D. Janicaud, *La Puissance du rationnel* (Paris, Gallimard, 1985).

nature, one insists upon the technological conquest and exploitation of nature. In man's relationship to himself, especially men among themselves, one speaks of the democratization of societies. As for man's relationship with what is above him, with the divine, one finds a variety of terms: "secularization"[2]; or "the disenchantment of the world" (*Entzauberung der Welt*) (Max Weber)[3]; or "the eclipse of God" (M. Buber)[4]; or the "de-divinzation" or "flight of the gods" (*Entgötterung*) (Heidegger)[5]; and finally "the death of God" (Nietzsche). As the reader can tell, I cite the phrases in no particular order, without claiming that it is an exhaustive list. Nor do I seek to parse their meanings, nor to pronounce upon the validity of the interpretations they convey. I merely want to recall one interpretation, or impression, that is widely shared: the withdrawal of the sacred.

I want to treat the problem posed by this withdrawal. To do so, I will reflect upon a text much older than those of the authors I just mentioned. It is found at the beginning of the period we customarily call "modern." It is from St. John of the Cross (1542–1591) and belongs to the second half of the sixteenth century.[6] It is found in the *Ascent of Mt. Carmel*, in a chapter

2   See the synthesis of G. Marramao, art. "Säkularisation," *Historisches Wörterbuch der Philosophie*, t. 8, 1992, col. 1133–1161.
3   The most well-known text of M. Weber is doubtlessly the conference "Wissenschaft als Beruf" (1922), found in *Schriften zur Wissenschaftslehre*, ed. M. Sukale (Stuttgart, Reclam, 1991), pp. 250–251. See as well, M. Gauchet, *Le Désenchantement du monde. Une histoire politique de la religion* (Paris, Gallimard, 1985).
4   M. Buber, *Gottesfinsternis* [1952], in *Werke* (Munich, Kösel and Heidelberg, Lambert Schneider, 1963), t. 1, pp. 505–603.
5   M. Heidegger, "Die Zeit des Weltbildes," in *Holzwege* (Francfort, Klostermann, 1950), p. 70.
6   I cite from: Saint John of the Cross, *Subida del monte Carmelo*, II, 22, *Obras completas*, ed. L. Ruano de la Iglesia (Madrid, Biblioteca de autores cristianos, 1989 [12th edition])), pp. 199–207 (henceforth, SMC).

sometimes called "one of the most grandiose" of this work.[7] I can treat it separately because the author himself considers it a useful digression, but not strictly indispensable to his purpose.[8]

2. A stingy grace?

The guiding question of this text is none other than the right way of experiencing God, the experience that modernity seems to deny to us. Here it is precisely a question of words and the Word; the former are denigrated for the sake of the last. John begins with a counterattack that seals the absence of the divine by changing it into an interdiction: "It is not God's will that souls should desire to receive by a supernatural path determinate visions or words. . . ."[9]

What is here condemned is nothing less than what is popularly called "mysticism." For the man in the street, a "mystic" is someone who sees or understands divine things that others cannot perceive, and which are novel, "un-heard-of." In this sense, John of the Cross is not a mystic and, what is more, he does not want to be one.[10] Then an objection is posed, in scholastic terms a *sed contra*, which leads to an impasse: the practice of asking for visions was licit in what John calls "the old Law." Moreover, not only was it licit to ask God to speak, but since God himself required it, not to do so was wrong. It is this last point, and it alone, that John illustrates. He cites in Latin, and translates into

7   Hans U. von Balthasar, *La Gloire et la Croix. Les aspects esthétiques de la Révélation*, II, Styles, 2. De Jean de la Croix à Péguy (Paris, Aubier, 1972), p. 60.

8   I have not found very much secondary literature to assist the beginner that I am. G. Morel, *Le Sens de l'existence selon saint Jean de la Croix* (Paris, Aubier, 1965), t. 2, pp. 186–87, is rather brief. Some very fine formulations can be found in J. Baruzi, *Saint Jean de la Croix et le problème de l'expérience mystique* (Paris, Alcan, 1924), pp. 526–27.

9   SMC, #2, p. 200.

10   See Z. Werblowski, "On the mystical rejection of mystical illuminations. A note on the non-cogntiive mysticism of St. John of the Cross" [Hebrew], *Iyyun*, 14, 1963, pp. 205–12.

Castillan, two passages, and recalls (without naming them) Moses and King David, and finally "ancient priests and prophets." All these passages show that the characters of the Old Testament did not hesitate to ask God to speak; in fact, God himself required it.

> Thus, we have seen . . . and concluded from the witnesses of Holy Scripture . . . that this was practiced under the old law, thus that it was permitted, even commanded, by God. And when they failed to do so, God scolded them. . . . Thus we see in Holy Scripture that Moses constantly consulted God, as did David and the other kings of Israel . . . and the ancient priests and prophets, and God answered them and spoke to them without becoming angry, so they did well in so doing. If they had failed to do so, it would have been a defect – which is true. Why, therefore, would it not be good to do so today under the new law of grace, as it was done yesterday?[11]

One can observe that John limited himself to one of the two modes of knowledge he began by referring to. Now, it is only a matter of asking for words from God, not *things* to see. Why? Perhaps because it would have been more difficult to find examples of God wanting someone to ask him for something to see. The king Hezekiah asked for a sign (which he in fact received), but he did so on his own initiative (II *Kings,* 20, 8–11; = *Isaiah,* 38, 22. 7.). In any case, "to see God" is both dangerous and difficult (*Exodus,* 33, 20). However, the main reason for the narrowing operated by John is that it prepares his reflection upon the Word of God, the *Logos,* and that he is hastening to attain his true object.

Be that as it may, the old alliance as presented by John is characterized by a greater familiarity between God and men. To speak to God and to hear him speak are not extraordinary. Man and God are on an equal footing with one another. The divine seems permanently available. One could even say he weighs heavily upon the human scene, that he insists upon manifesting himself and intervening.

11 *SMC,* #2, p. 200.

Since John ends his examples with a vague enumeration, I will permit myself to generalize also. In the old alliance, God seems closer to man than in the new alliance. He intervenes by deeds that are more easily "read" as divine than those reported by the New Testament. His exploits are more spectacular. Medieval Jewish apologetics knew how to make hay of this argument: the liberation of the people held captive in Egypt, the scourges that struck the Egyptians, crossing the Red Sea, manna coming down from heaven for forty years – miracles that occurred before six hundred thousand witnesses – are hardly deniable.[12] Whether these events really happened or not, the narrative of them is much more grandiose than anything the New Testament offers: healings of individuals, miracles done among a small circle, thus without much in the way of witnesses, the resurrection of Jesus itself, which no one saw occur, even if witnesses claimed to have seen the resurrected one appear to them. The Old Testament contains much more that is "marvelous" than the New Testament, which seems in comparison rather flat. The observation has been often made, starting with the Church Fathers who spoke of the "humble manner of speech" (*sermo humilis*) of the New Testament.[13]

In his own way, John of the Cross recognizes the same fact, or an analogous fact, to the one that characterizes the modern period. He acknowledges (at least implicitly, since he does not thematize the phenomenon) something that allow me to speak of the "modernity" of the New Testament. And this "modernity" does not have a positive connotation, certainly not for the man in the street of our societies, who associates "modern" with "progress" and "improvement." Quite the contrary. The New Testament has something that is more sober, grayer, than the Old. One is tempted to think that the distance between the Old Testament and certain aspects of "paganism" is less than is ordinarily believed, in

12 See, for example, Jehuda Halévi, *Kuzari*, I, # 83–88, ed. D. Baneth-H. Ben Shammai (Jérusalem, Magnes, 1977), pp. 22–25.
13 See E. Auerbach, "Sacrae scripturae sermo humilis" [in French], in *Écrits sur Dante* (Paris, Macula, 1998), pp. 221–29.

this case concerning the open and free relations between the divine and the human.

John of the Cross recognizes a paradox: the new law seems to be the opposite of a progress over the old law, rather a regress. The divine is not brought closer, but distanced. The fullness of revelation represents a disenchantment. To add to the injury: what was formerly permitted is henceforth forbidden. Nonetheless, as John underlines, it is truly a "law of grace" which opens an "era of grace."[14] Grace, however, is apparently more severe than the Law which was merely law. Gift (*kharis*), far from giving superabundantly, seems to withdraw.

3. The definitive religion

Confronting this enigma, John proposes his solution:

> To which one must reply that the principal reason why the requests made to God were permitted in the law of Scripture, and why it was fitting that the prophets and the priests desired visions and revelations from God, was because the faith was not yet so well founded, nor the evangelical law established. Therefore, they needed to ask of God and He to speak, sometimes by words, sometimes by visions and revelations, other times in figures and images, and in many other manners of communication. Because everything that He answered, spoke, and revealed were the mysteries of our faith and the things it concerns and which it addresses. . . . But now that faith in Christ is given and the evangelical law is manifested in this era of grace, there is no need to inquire in this way, nor that He speak or respond as before. For by giving us, as He has done, His Son, His unique Word – there is no other – He has spoken and revealed all things at one time in one Word. There is no need to speak further.[15]

John's response is that the period of direct contact between

14 *SMC*, #2–3, p. 200.
15 SMC, #3, pp. 200–201.

God and men in the history of Revelation represented a provision-al stage, where everything was still ill-"founded" or "established." This answer is obviously the answer, the classic answer, that a Christian must give. And without doubt John of the Cross is a Christian of perfect orthodoxy; he is even more, a Doctor of the Church. We therefore are not surprised to read from his pen a summary of the doctrine of the Fathers of the Church on the rela-tionship between the Old and the New Testaments. The Old is the prefiguration of the New, it is ordained (*enderezada*) to the latter. Hence his insistence upon the language of sign, type, and symbol (*figures y semejanzas*). Now, however, God has clearly said what he wanted to say and there is nothing more to say to us.

In this way, it is Christianity that is responsible for something that we must call "the flight of the sacred." John of the Cross is not the only one to say this. An idea of this sort can be found later, for example, among authors who probably never read him. It is implicit in many authors and explicit in Nietzsche. With him, however, its meaning has changed significance: what was positive for John is negative for Nietzsche. His confession of faith will be recast as an accusation. More neutral authors have connected the "secularization of the world" with Christianity, as well as with the earlier critique by Israel's prophets of the worship of the powers of nature. In this way, they sought to explain the withdrawal of the sacred, not by a series of external facts having nothing to do with the religious domain, e.g., the Enlightenment, or the ration-alization connected to capitalism, but by developments within the very center of this domain. I have Max Weber and Marcel Gauchet in mind. One cannot but be struck by the fact that the same answer is given by John of the Cross, not merely within "the religious sphere," but from within Christianity itself.

To this point, John's response consists in the following: reve-lation is ended, there will be no other. To this one can observe that at this level of generality his answer, that of a Christian, is only a particular version of the claim raised by other religions to be the last, the most perfect, the definitive, religion. The three religions that claim Abraham present themselves as unsurpassable. Now, they justify this claim by different arguments, but all of these depend upon the idea they construct of what religion in general must be. The clearest example of this type of attitude in the Christian domain is, without doubt, Hegel's, who sees in Christianity the "absolute religion" and tries to show that it is in Christianity that the religion corresponds best to it concept.[16] The experts in the concrete history of phenomena said to be 'religious" have no trouble in showing that the general concept of religion with which he worked was in fact derived from Christianity, more or less self-consciously.

All the religions that appeal to Abraham attempt to present themselves as final and definitive. This is especially the case with Islam. Mohammed seems to have had a vivid awareness of his position in history, and of the problem posed by his coming into a world in which Judaism and Christianity had already spread. It was necessary to show how a prophetic message could claim to be authentic without being superfluous because of those that preceded it. In any event, this is how Islam generally interprets the Quranic saying according to which Mohammed is the "seal of the prophets" (*hatam* [s.v.l.] *al-nabiyyîn*)" (*Quran*, 33, 40).[17] While not certain, it is possible that the formulation, and therefore the claim that it makes to be the final stage of revelation, is older than Islam itself. It occurs in Tertullian, where it designates Christ, and al-Biruni cites it in a text of Mani, the founder of Manicheanism.[18] In any case, the commentators belonging to the

16 G. W. F. Hegel, *Vorlesungen über die Philosophie der Religion*, in *Sämtliche Werke*, Jubiläumsausgabe, ed. H. Glockner (Stuttgart, Frommann, 1928), t. 15, p. 99.

17 For the expression, see C. Colpe, Das *Siegel der Propheten: historische Beziehungen zwischen Judentum, Judenchristentum, Heidentum und frühem Islam* (Berlin, Institut Kirche und Judentum (ANZ, 3), 1990), pp. 227–43; and G. Stroumsa, "Le sceau des prophètes: la nature d'une métaphore manichéenne," in *Savoir et Salut* (Paris, Le Cerf, 1992), pp. 275–88.

18 Tertullian, *Adversus Judaeos*, VIII, 12, ed. E. Kroymann, CCSL, II-2 (Turnhout, 1954), p. 1361, 97; al-Biruni, *The Chronology of Ancient*

dominant school of interpretation adopt the reading of *hatam*, "seal," instead of *hatim*, "he who binds (and confirms)," and thus understand that Mohammed is the last (*akhir*) of the prophets.[19] In order to firm up what remains somewhat obscure in the Quran, various sayings of Mohammed (*hadith*) are conveyed that would have stated unambiguously that no prophet will come after him. Among these sayings is a parable, that of a house built by a man, which is beautiful in every way except that it lacks a brick. Mohammed is likened to the brick that makes the edifice perfect.[20]

Biblical Judaism and the Talmud affirm the eternal character of the Law of Moses, although not always very clearly. It appears never to have had the concern to prove the definitive character of this Law before it encountered Christianity and Islam.[21] Then we see it deploy a series of arguments, both extrinsic and intrinsic. Thus Maimonides argues that the eternity of the Law derives from the eternity of what is promised to Israel, since it is the fulfillment of the commandments that inhibits the disappearance of the people.[22] This is an extrinsic argument. But the stronger argument is intrinsic, even if it requires lengthy developments. It basically consists in showing that the Law is, as Psalm 19 puts it, "perfect" (*torath YHWH temimah*). Perfection is understood as the impossibility of adding or subtracting anything from it. Perfection implies that adding would mean excess and subtracting, defect.[23]

Nations [. . .], ed. E. Sachau (Francfort, Minerva, 1969 [London, 1879]), p. 190.

19 See Y. Friedmann, "Finality of Prophethood in Sunni Islam," *Jerusalem Studies in Arabic and Islam*, 7, 1986, pp. 177–215.

20 The references can be found in A. J. Wensinck et al., *Concordance et indices de la tradition musulmane*, Leyde, t. VI, 1967–68, pp. 88b–89a. See especially Muslim, *Sahih*, book 43 (Fadâ'il), Bab 7, #20–23 (Le Caire, 1955), t. 4, pp. 1790–91.

21 See W. Z. Harvey, art. "Torah (Eternity [or Non-Abrogability])," *Encyclopaedia Judaica* (Jerusalem, Keter, 1992), t. 15, col. 1244–46.

22 Maimonides, *Guide des égarés*, II, 29, ed. Joël, p. 240.

23 *Ibid.*, p. 269, cf. 303.

The perfection of the Law owes, first, to its source, the perfect prophet, the one in whom all the faculties of the soul are at their maximum purity, and, second, its results, to wit: social and spiritual utility.

As for Christianity, its apologetic effort bears above all on the demonstration of the way in which it fulfills the Old Covenant. John of the Cross adds nothing on this score, but he does have the merit of formulating the problem posed for every religion by the fact of the end, or closure, of revelation. This, quite simply, is the fact that "religion" is a revelation. He affirms this fundamental datum without particular fanfare, so much does it go without saying. We are the ones who have to find in it matter for thought. "The things of faith are not from man but from the mouth of God Himself."[24] What is here expressed is the fundamental conception that a religion has to have of the divine; it is almost a definition, or at least a characterization, of what a God must be. It is proper to the divine that he alone is able to say that he is the divine. Pascal wrote: "God speaks well of God."[25] One has to go so far as to say that God alone can say, "I am God." If this is so, religion cannot be the work of man, and if a word is to be said to be divine, it is God who must speak it. And this is something that cannot occur except at some determinate moment in the history of human beings.

4. A God reduced to silence

John supports his claim, which until then was made without any appeal to authority, by a biblical citation.

> This is the meaning of the text in which St. Paul wants to induce the Hebrews not to follow their previous ways and manners of dealing with God according to the Law of Moses, but to only rest their gaze upon Christ. He says: "What God said formerly to our fathers in diverse ways

24 *SMC*, #3, p. 200.
25 Pascal, *Pensées*, #799, *op. cit.*, t. 3, p. 237.

and manners, now, in these last days, he spoke to us in his Son," all in one time.[26]

As one can see, he quotes and comments upon the first sentence of the *Letter to the Hebrews*. He does not add anything new to the text, but contents himself with explicating an idea that the passage does not spell out: "in one time" (*de una vez*). In fact, he lets the text comment upon itself only because it is the text itself that insists, several times, that the event of salvation in Christ took place "only one time" (*ephapax*) (9, 26–28; cf. 7, 27; 9, 12; 10, 10), texts that have been used time and time again by those who seek to contrast two types of temporality, one that is pagan and cyclical, the other biblical and linear.

But John then adds an idea that is not found in the text he bases himself upon, nor to my knowledge in the New Testament itself:

> In this way, the Apostle lets it be understood that God has remained, as it were, mute, and that he has nothing more to say, because what he was saying in fragments by the prophets, he said in its entirety, by giving us the Whole who is his son.[27]

The novelty of this idea doubtlessly explains the prudence with which it is formulated. The "Apostle" (St. Paul, who was taken at the time for the author of the Epistle) "lets it be understood" something that John expresses in an extraordinary, and even schocking formula: God "has remained, as it were, mute" (*ha quedado como mudo*). What John adds is the idea of God's silence. To be sure, it is an old idea, one that has remained current and relevant, often formulated as an accusation launched against a Heaven that fails to respond, for example, in the face of human suffering. It is already found in the Bible, in the *Psalms* for example (28, 1; 35, 22; 83, 2; 109, 1), the Prophets (*Isaiah*, 64, 11; *Habbakuh*, 1, 13), or in the book of *Job* (30, 20). In a passage of *Isaiah*, God is even deemed to recognize that he has closed his

26 *SMC*, #4, p. 201.
27 *Ibid.*

mouth (57, 19). But in truth the dialogue with man is never interrupted. In contrast, in modern times a new attitude appears: man cloaks himself in a haughty silence vis-à-vis the silence of God. The famous strophe that Alfred de Vigny added to his poem "The mount of Olives" is well known:

> If it is true that in the sacred Garden of the Scriptures
> That the Son of man said what is reported;
> Mute, blind and deaf to the cry of creatures,
> If Heaven leaves us as an aborted world,
> The just man will oppose disdain to the absence
> And will only respond with chilly silence
> To the eternal silence of the divinity.[28]

The spirited response of Simone Weil is less well known: Vigny "didn't have the right to say what the response of the just is to this silence, because he wasn't just. The just person loves. The one who is capable not only of listening but also of loving understands this silence as the word of God."[29]

For John of the Cross, the silence of God, his "mutism," is the *consequence* of the fact that he already has said Everything. In the paragraph that interests us here, he takes yet another step beyond what came before, even vis-à-vis the biblical passage of which he claims to give a free translation. In substance, the *Letter to the Hebrews* affirms that God has said in the Son everything that he said in fragments by the prophets. This could mean that God decided to give us a certain message. And this message, to be sure, could very well be all that he wanted to say to us. But it is not necessarily *everything*, absolutely speaking. In the past, it was delivered in dribs and drabs, piecemeal, now it has been transmitted in its integrity. It is perhaps in this sense that the Bible distinguishes (in a passage that is not entirely clear) "the hidden things" (*nistaroth*) that belong to God and the "revealed things" (*nigloth*)

---

28 A. de Vigny, *Les Destinées*, ed. de 1862.
29 S. Weil, "L'amour de Dieu et le malheur," in *Oeuvres, op. cit.*, p. 715.

which were confided to Israël so that it could practice them (*Deut.*, 29, 28). John of the Cross, however, goes further. He affirms, quite deliberately, that God has given us, purely and simply, Everything (he employs the majuscule [*dandonos al Todo*]). God retains nothing for himself, he gives without reserve everything he is. God is now poor, as it were, nothing remains to be given.

God, therefore, has nothing more to say, since he has said everything. How is this possible? What John of the Cross affirms is not simply unique to him. Elsewhere one can find the idea according to which God has spoken in such a definitive and total way that he has become, as it were, the prisoner of what he said. God, as it is said, "has committed himself." One can cite, for example, the famous passage of the Talmud in which an assembly of sages decides on a majority vote, despite the indubitable miracles provided in favor of the opinion of one of the sages. In justification, it was recalled that no voice coming from heaven, no direct intervention of God, can prevail over the judgment of the wise, because, according to the Bible itself, the Law no longer belongs to heaven (*Deut.*, 30, 12) ("heaven" is understood to mean "next to God"). The Law has definitively come down to earth, where it is left to the discussion and decisions of the wise.[30]

5. The discourse of the God who is mute

The Christian response to this, the response of St. John of the Cross, does have something that is original to it: it is that what is given is not a law but a person; and that, moreover, this person is God. It is *in Christ* that God has already said everything to us, and therefore has nothing more to say. John's answer does not speak of Christianity, therefore, merely to show that it constitutes the definitive religion. He speaks of something else, the *object* of Christian faith. It is by this, moreover, that one recognizes he is a Christian.

30 Babylonian Talmud, *Baba Metsiah*, 59b. This text was commented on by Gershom Scholem, *Über einige Grundbegriffe des Judentums* (Francfort, Suhrkamp, 1970), p. 104.

One can recognize a non-Christian by the various ways in which he is interested in "Christianity." He can be interested in it to refute it, to narrate its history, even to demonstrate its civilizing value. Ten years before Andrew Sullivan, I amused myself in another book by calling "Christianist" the person who develops this sort of theory.[31] I wanted to distinguish him from the "Christian" who is interested, not in Christianity, but in Christ. In the same way, a Jew is interested in the Law of Moses, not in Judaism.

John continues:

> This is why the person who would now ask God, or who would want to see a vision or receive some revelation, not only commits a error, but injures God, by not fixing his eyes wholly on Christ, without wishing for any other thing or novelty.[32]

If God, *per impossibile*, spoke again, this would be to repeat himself, to harp. Now, it is this impossibility that John next attributes to God, employing a figure of speech that used to be well-known, prosopopoeia. And the one he has speak is none other than God: "God could respond to him in this way, saying. . . ." Here it is not the Trinity, but God the Father, who speaks. This is an boldness that is rather rare in Christianity. In the plastic arts, for example, Christianity does not really like to represent the Father apart from the Son, as if he were visible apart from the latter. After all, He has given himself entirely to the Son.

> If I said everything in my Word, who is my Son, I have no other that I now could say or reveal that would be more than that one. Pay attention to him alone, because I have said and revealed everything in him.[33]

What God the Father is made to say in the passage above is

31 See my work, *Eccentric Culture. A Theory of Western civilization* (South Bend, St Augustine's Press,), p. 143.
32 *SMC*, #5, p. 201.
33 *Ibid.*

nothing but a repetition of what John has just said in his own name. The speech of the Father illustrates and confirms a teaching already given. And the content of this teaching is that the discourse that John puts on God's lips is impossible. In the passage, God speaks. And he does so in order to say that he cannot speak any more. The content of the message is its own impossibility. Here one approximates certain well known logical paradoxes, such as when one says "I am not speaking at this moment."

II. The silence of the flesh

Be that as it may, the Father's speech above does contain some new elements, attending to them will allow us to more precisely grasp the teaching given until now.

1. *Whoever wants more, really wants less*
In the first paragraph of God's discourse John introduces a clever counterpoint concerning the word and idea of "more" (*más*).

> Look at him alone . . . and you will find even more than you ask me for and more than you could desire.[34]

This play on words will continue through the entirety of the prosopopeia of the Father. According to John, God cannot say *more* than he has already said, he has nothing *more* to give:

> [God] has spoken to us and revealed all things, once for all, by this Word and he has nothing more to say.

> What can I now answer you or reveal to you that would be more than that?

> [God] has no more faith to reveal, nor will he ever have more.[35]

34 *Ibid.*
35 SMC, #3, p. 201; #5, p. 201; #7, p. 202.

But in what he has given, that is, in Christ, one can find more than what one asks for or desires:

You have nothing more to ask me, nor to desire, of revelations or visions on my part. Look intently at him, you will find all of that already done and given – and even more.

> If you wish for me to declare hidden things, or events, to you, only cast your eyes on him and you will find in him the most hidden mysteries, as well as the wisdom and marvels of God contained in him. . . . These treasures of wisdom will be much more sublime, more savory, and more useful to you than what you wish to know. . . . And if you still want other divine or corporal visions or revelations, look at him in his humanity, and you will find in him more than you think, because the Apostle also says that the plenitude of the divinity abides corporeally in Christ.[36]

Let us risk a somewhat bombastic formulation. According to John, there is *more* in what has already occurred than in what could occur, *more* than already happened. To add something to what already is, would in fact be to detract from it. This is a paradox found in a number of contexts. For example, in Plotinus. For the neoplatonist, the perfection of a level of being is measured by its simplicity. To add something to one of these levels would be therefore to demote it, adding ballast that would cause it to fall to another level.[37] I can therefore venture an initial response to the paradox indicated above concerning the grace which, instead of adding, retires. To understand it, one can make use of what we learn in aesthetic experience, making use of the idea of "grace" that is – here we have to use a verbal play that is more than playful – "gracious." What is gracious is that which the slightest addition would spoil.

We start with the fact that there is more in what is given than in what is desired. Desire (*erôs*) since Plato is understood as what

36 *SMC*, #5–6, p. 202.
37 Plotinus, *Enneads*, III, 8 [30], 11, 13; V, 5 [32], 13, 10; VI, 7 [38], 41, 16–17.

transcends everything that is already there, as the eternal dissatis-faction before what is usually too quickly called "the given."[38] Here on the contrary, when it is truly a matter of a gift, the desire is transcended from the beginning. The recipient finds himself inca-pable of rising to the height of what is offered to him. Desire leaves something to desire. In this optic, certain paradoxes of the Gospel can be illumined, for example, "he who seeks, finds, he who asks, receives" (*Matth.*, 7, 8, etc.) This does not mean, as some are tempted to think, that whoever really looks will find, according to the Latin phrase, *labor omnia vincit improbus* – diligent labor will overcome.[39] One must take the Gospel phrase at its literal mean-ing, with the entire force that the present tense gives it: not "he who seeks will find,", but rather ". . . finds." If the object of desire is already there, it is as if we find ourselves submerged in it. Since it has found us, we need only to seek to find it. More prosaically, we just need to note that we always find ourselves within it.

According to an opposite paradox, to ask for more faith as though the faith that we have been given was deficient, would be to demonstrate the deficiency of one's faith:

> [God continues to speak:] But now whoever asks me and wishes that I would answer him, or that I would reveal something to him, that would be tantamount to asking me again for Christ, and asking me for more faith and imply-ing that there is a defect in the faith (*ser falto en ella*) that has already been given in Christ; in this way he would greatly insult my beloved Son; because in so asking, he would be lacking in faith (*le faltaria en la fe*).[40]

This "more faith" that would be asked for is not the addition of confidence that the father of the possessed mute young man asked Christ to grant him: "I believe, help my unbelief!" (*Mark*, 9, 24). It would be to add another object of faith.

38 Plato, *Symposium*, 200e
39 The Latin proverb comes from Virgil, *Georgics*, I, 145–46.
40 SMC, #5, pp. 201–2.

2. *Without return*

The mistake is actually double:

> ... and thus, he would greatly insult my beloved Son; not only because he would be lacking in faith, but he would in effect oblige him to become incarnate again and to relive his first life and death.[41]

What John envisages is something like an eternal return of the same. The example that the stoics sometimes gave of this doctrine was that of the trial and death of Socrates, once again accused by Anytus, once again drinking the hemlock.[42] It is as if John is enlarging the well-known parallel between Socrates and Jesus, by applying to Jesus the idea of eternal return. But he does so to reject the idea. Merely to articulate it, suffices to demonstrate its absurdity. Still, one can say that John of the Cross is in deeper agreement with Nietzsche than one might think, at least if one understands "the eternal return of the same" (*ewige Wiederkehr des Gleichen*) as imposing upon us the thought of the absolute irreversibility of life, the fact that each instant – coinciding with an infinity of instants that, because of the return, cannot be said to be "other" – has an infinite weight.

In this passage, John performs a brutal *reductio ad adsurdum*, destined to lay bare the logic of the attitude he is criticizing. To ask for a particular revelation is to ask God to have his Son incarnate and die once again. To ask more from God would be to ask him for what he has already done. To ask for something else would be to ask for the same thing, once more. This is an inevitable consequence of the fact that God has nothing more to give than he has already given, once for all time. One cannot leave what is everything. If you wanted to, you would return to it. To add to the totality, would be to repeat it. But God only knows how to give everything. To ask him for anything is therefore to ask for that in which, or rather: he in whom, he has already given everything.

41 *Ibid.*
42 See Origen, *Contre Celse*, IV, #67, ed. M. Borret, *Sources chrétiennes*, n. 136 (Paris, Le Cerf, 1968), p. 350.

John leads every possible gift back to Christ. In him are contained "all the treasures of the divinity" (*Col.*, 2, 3). It is in him that one, necessarily, has to seek for what God has to give.

Now, what is given is a totality, like an organism in which the part cannot exist without the whole, and not a sum of parts that are external to one another. The gift of God is concentrated in, and unified and singularized, by the unsubstitutable individuality of one human life and death. This is characterized by an irreversible unfolding. Perhaps this is what John indicates by the expression "to pass through life" (*pasar por la vida*). It is such a "passing through" that makes of human life something other than a simple "having life," which elevates it to the status of *bios*, which has a history, the content of which is rightly called a "biography."

The process by which the gift of God is singularized, that is, its concentration in a singular human life, allows one to avoid a problem that otherwise would come up. This is the problem – a very practical one – of the end of the communication, often expressed as follows: "over and out!" How to know that God has said everything? If God has to say that he has finished speaking, he must speak in order to do so, which leads to what we might call "an infinite regress." In other words, logically speaking, can the definitive character of the revelation be a part of the revealed message? Can a revealed message say: "the present message is the last?" However, if the revealed "datum" is a human person, the problem does not pose itself, there is no need, within the message, to indicate that it is the last, and that nothing will come afterwards. If the message is nothing else but the one who expresses it, then the "end" of the message coincides with the death of the message-messenger.

Here John draws out the consequence that remained implicit in the way in which the New Testament resolved the question – one quite important for every historical religion – of its definitive character. Above, we saw that Islam had its prophet say that no other would come after him. For it, as well as, *mutandis mutatis*, for Judaism, it was a question of making the divine law immune from either abrogation or a purported "correction" by addition or subtraction. The New Testament puts in Christ's mouth analogous warnings against those who will come and announce the end of time. Those, however, against whom one must be on guard say nothing other than "I am the Christ" (*Matth.*, 24, 5, et cet.). They do not pretend to add to Christ but to be Christ himself, returned. There is no one else to come. Christianity cannot conceive of someone who would come who would not be the Christ. History is closed, or circular: what will come is nothing other than the return in glory of the one who has already come, once for all time. "He who must come" (*Matth.*, 11, 3) is none other than the one who has come. This is because for Christianity, only Christ, strictly speaking, has *come*. He alone came from elsewhere ("from above"). All others, real or possible, past or future, cannot, strictly speaking, come. At most they could emerge from what is already there: the world, humanity, history. In principle, they *are* already there.

3. *The incarnate Word*

John of the Cross here supposes that the reader knows certain absolutely central points of Catholic doctrine that, for this reason, he does not need to explain. It seems to me that for this same reason, today one needs to spell them out, especially since we have arrived at the point in his discussion when this teaching, until now presupposed, is presented in all its amplitude. John has mentioned "his Son (the Son of God the Father), who is His word – and there is no other." Later, it is the Father who mentions "my word, who is my Son."[43] The identification of Jesus Christ with the Word of God and thus to the eternal Son, the second Person of the Trinity, is obviously essential to Christianity. It is the theological elaboration of certain declarations of the New Testament, above all of the Prologue to the Gospel of St. John, where it is spoken of "the Word who became flesh" (1, 14). This word is not any-old word, even though divine. It is "at the beginning" (as the obvious

43 *SMC*, #3, p. 201 and #4, p. 201.

parallel with *Genesis* has it), the word through which God created everything, and therefore cannot itself be a creature.

This identification has a major consequence concerning the status of Christ. On occasion, John speaks of what Jesus Christ taught, hence what he said.[44] But this is only an initial formulation, which does not go to the heart of things. For him, Christ is not someone who speaks, but who is spoken. He is not the announcer of a message, a sort of prophet. He himself is the message. He is everything that God says and has to say. There is no distance between the messenger and the message, but rather a perfect identity. What is said is not only a collection of words, but a life and a personality that mutually illumine each other: the life flowing from the initial decision of the personality, manifesting the personality. Hence the personality furnishes the key which allows one to correctly understand the meaning of both the words and the deeds of Christ.

The "word" therefore is not something purely verbal; it is an act at the same time it is a word. And even what Christ will say must be understood as an action more than a description of what is, less as teachings than as clarifications brought to the deeds or the whole composed of Christ's attitude and life. Thus, the Sermon on the Mount, with the rules of life that are put forth in it and which are, strictly speaking, inapplicable, is less a "new law" than the presentation of the interior attitude of Christ, which attitude illumines his conduct, culminating in the Passion. Every word of Christ is a way of saying who he is and has to converge toward the "I am" that St. John's Gospel has him pronounce several times in particularly significant occasions. This is a deliberate echo of the divine name given to Moses at the burning bush (*Exodus*, 3, 14).

Many sayings of Christ are reported. The synoptic Gospels, as well as apocryphal ones, are full of them. We also can recall the collection of sayings of Jesus not found in these texts, what are called the *logia agrapha* (the unwritten words). Among all these

44 *SMC*, #7, p. 202.

words, John of the Cross, in the passage I am dealing with now, only cites one:

> For when Christ says on the + these words – *consummatum est* – when he expired, not only did these ancient forms come to an end, but also all the ceremonies and customs of the old law.[45]

Juan de Yepes chose to cite these words, as it were, by signing it with the name he chose when entering religious life. The *consummatum est* was recounted by the author of the fourth Gospel, who was known to him under the name of "John." In that Gospel, they were the very last words of Jesus, pronounced from the cross. In taking his religious name, Juan of Yepes did not actually write the word "cross" but he sketched a little cross, the cross whose name he wanted to bear.[46] This "signature" – what the illiterate would write – was not simply a sign of humility on his part. It fits perfectly with what its origin indicates, that is, "the word of the cross" (1 Corinthians 1, 18). This word is *consummatum est* (in Greek, *tetelestai*) (*John* 19, 30). This is a strange word, not even a sentence but an isolated verb, its subject unknown, a declaration without content. It doubtlessly is the interpretation the author of the fourth Gospel made of what was reported by the three synoptic Gospels.

According to them, the last word of Christ on the cross was nothing but a "great cry" (*phônè megalè*), one that was "emitted" or "cried out," thus inarticulate, and followed by death (unless it was this death itself) (*Matth.* 27, 50; *Mark* 15, 37). We could say that the last word of the Word lacks intelligible meaning. This word is only a voice, a sound pronounced by the vocal organs of an animal.[47] One produced at the moment when his lungs were emptied. This sound was produced by flesh, therefore, it was

45 *Ibid.*
46 For the significance of this practice, see B. Teuber, *Sacrificium litterae – Allegorische Rede und mystische Erfahrung in der Dichtung des heiligen Johannes vom Kreuz* (Munich, Wilhelm Fink, 2003), pp. 505–17.
47 See Aristotle, *History of Animals*, IV, 9, 535b4.

nothing but the spasm of flesh reacting against itself. There is nothing in it that transcends the flesh, that moves it toward the spiritual dimension of man. In fact, the sound of the one who "renders his spirit" is the sign and seal of the irrevocable departure of this dimension. It is the sign of the abolition of the distance that allows for meaning and significance. At this point of time, the Word and the flesh are but one. In the simplest, least "theological" meaning of the phrase, the word becomes flesh.

The last word of the Word is that of an impotent Word, reduced to silence. The power of the word is here the silence of the Word, stripped of all power. But here, everything is turned upside-down. What would be the defeat of a speaker that one had silenced, is no longer that if the speaker is identical with what he has to say, if he *is* the word of another who speaks him. It is not the word that speaks but the speaking subject, the speaker. If, therefore, a man is the Word, the Word par excellence, he ought to be silent. More precisely, what would be the most "revealing" in him, or what would be, as we say, the most "meaningful," would not be what he says, but what he does.

It is, therefore, unreasonable to regret the silence of the divine. This silence is the inevitable consequence of a word uttered without reserve. Christ on the Mount of Olives, in Vigny's poem cited above, has no response to expect. He himself *is* the response of God. This is recognized, in another context, by the central character – one who is resolutely "pagan" – in what is probably C. S. Lewis's best novel: "I know now, Lord, why you utter no answer: you are yourself the answer."[48] The silence of God gives rise to complaints against him, even accusations. But this sort of accusation only desires to inflict upon him a reproach and a vengeance that he has already fully suffered. A character in a novel by Bernanos says this magnificently:

> . . . if our God were that of pagans or philosophers (for
> me, it's the same thing), he could very well find refuge in

48 C. S. Lewis, *Till we have faces. A myth retold* [1956] (Grand Rapids, Eerdmans, 1966), p. 308.

the highest heavens, our misery would cause him to fall from there. But you know that our God stepped forth and came before us. You can show him the finger, spit on his face, whip him, and, finally, nail him to a cross. Whatever. It's already been done.[49]

4. The Trinity

The identification of the Word with the Son, presupposed by John of the Cross, in turn presupposes the Trinity. That is obvious. For the first time, the saint brings together the names of the three persons, Father, Son, and Holy Spirit, in the paragraph I am commenting on.

> From the time I descended with my Spirit on him on Mt. Tabor, saying: Behold, my beloved Son, in whom I am well pleased, I have ceased all these ways of instruction and of responding, and have given all things over to him.[50]

The Gospel passage he refers to concerns the Transfiguration (*Matthew.*, 17, 5). But John adds some words that are not found in the account ("I descended with my Spirit on him."). They suggest that he was reading it in conjunction with another passage, the scene of the baptism of Jesus by John the Baptist (*Matthew.*, 3, 16), a passage that is often interpreted, both in exegesis and in the plastic arts, as the presentation of the three persons of the Trinity.

John does not develop a theology of the Trinity. But he presupposes as known (by faith) what this doctrine serves to explain. For the Father to give Everything, to give his Word, to give His Son, does *not* signify giving something other than himself, and remaining the external witness of this gift. This is so clear to John himself that he can allow himself a somewhat loose formulation of it. In the passage, he presents an impossible state of affairs, that "I

49 G. Bernanos, *Journal d'un curé de campagne*, in *Oeuvres Romanesques*, ed. A. Béguin (Paris, Gallimard, 1961), p. 1162.
50 *SMC*, #5, p. 201.

ceased" (literally, "I raised my hand" (*alcé yo la mano*) all these ways of teaching and of responding. The formula gives the impression, if I can put it a bit disrespectfully, that God the Father would have "stepped aside," would have "retired from the business" in favor of his son who succeeded him. This, however, is a caricature with which many content themselves . . .

If there is anything that the Trinitarian doctrine makes impossible, it is this way of seeing things. The doctrine in question is not, first of all, a more or less arbitrary theory about the number of hypostases that compose the divine substance. It is above all an instrument which allows us to conceive of the personal engagement of God in the history of salvation, the adventure of God with men. One can summarize it in a phrase: God does not contract out. The Trinitarian doctrine attempts to articulate the identity and the difference between God and his incarnation, between the Father and the Son.

If God entered into history, it is necessary, first, that the Son be in some sense the same as the Father. Otherwise, the history of salvation would not personally engage God. He would remain, as it were, on the balcony, like the Homeric gods observing the battles of men. It would refer to someone who simply observed what happened, which concerned him not, except perhaps by means of an intermediary. The destiny of the incarnate Son, therefore, would not be the Father's own. To send the Son to suffer would be a way of putting himself at a distance. But, if there is to be an entrance of God in history, it is also necessary that the Father not be the Son, purely and simply. Otherwise, it would not be God who became incarnate. Becoming man, by that very token he would cease to be God. Or rather, he could not *become* man, but would be human from eternity, by his very nature, instead of entering the human realm – with all it entailed – by his free choice. And the history of Christ would not have its particular relevance.

John of the Cross only mentions briefly the third person of the Trinity, the Holy Spirit. He thus gives him the discrete place that objectively belongs to him. The Spirit given after Christ adds nothing to what was given once for all times. He is not a new object that was revealed, as if revelation was not completed with the mission of the Son. On the contrary, the Spirit recalls all that was done (*John* 14, 26).[51] He is, rather, he who gives, rather than he who is given. He is not a revealed object but a revealing subject. There are not two divine economies, one of the Word, which would be followed by the economy of the Spirit.[52]

III. After Everything

1. *What to do when all is said?*

Let us, therefore, suppose that everything has been said. What to do, then? First of all, we should note that this is not a totally idle question. This is not the first time that someone has thought that everything had been found already. La Bruyère's formulation "everything is said, at least since there were men, and they thought" is classic. And even in ancient Egypt, the scribe Khâ-kheper-Rê-seneb of the Middle Empire could ask himself the question, how he could write after so many great talents had done so?[53] And not too long ago, in a book that received a great deal of attention, an author combined Hegel with Leo Strauss and wrote of "the end of history."[54] But that everything has been said ought not to reduce us to silence. One, perhaps, can even say: on the contrary! Aristotle, for example, basing himself upon a cyclical notion of the progress of knowledge, wrote somewhere that

---

51 In a sense, the Félicité of Flaubert's *Un coeur simple* is right: the Spirit is as much a parrot as a dove...

52 This is the danger of the formulations of V. Lossky, *Essai sur la théologie mystique de l'Église d'Orient* (Paris, Le Cerf, 2005 [1944]), chapter VIII, pp. 153–69.

53 In A. H. Gardiner, *The Admonitions of an Egyptian Sage* (Leipzig, 1909), pp. 97–101 [*non vidi*], cited in J. Assmann, *Das kulturelle Gedächtnis. Schrift, Erinnerung und politische Identität in frühen Hochkulturen* (Beck, 1997 (2nd ed.)), pp. 97–8.

54 F. Fukuyama, *The End of History and the Last Man* (New York, The Free Press, 1992).

"almost all has already been discovered."[55] What remains is to collect it and to use it properly. Later, his disciple, the Arab thinker al-Farabi, wrote that philosophy has nothing more to seek since Aristotle, who brought it to its perfection. What remains, is to teach it as a certain science.[56]

Thus, if everything is *said*, a thousand things remain to be *done*. One can repeat the different steps or stages that led to the definitive word; one can also "deconstruct" the discourse, with or without the hope of arriving at an original evidence at the source of the discourse (the difference between the presence or absence of this hope being more or less what distinguishes the two versions of the idea of deconstruction, found in Heidegger and in Derrida); one can search another mode of expression, one closer to silence, at the extreme, coinciding with it. Finally, one can respond, in full awareness.

To be clear: the question I am posing here is *not* to know, in general, what to do when everything is said. It needs to be put more precisely: what to do when it is *God* who has said everything he has to say. And here, this "everything" signifies nothing less than everything that is (creation), or everything that God himself is. When one affirms that a definitive revelation has taken place, several possibilities are opened; one can sketch a typology of them.

Thus, the Jewish tradition affirms that the law of Moses is perfect. But it came to understand this perfection in the sense that it also comprehended, in advance, all the new interpretations that the sages of future generations were destined to propose. It further affirmed that the innovations of the scribes were revealed on Sinai. It also can entertain the thought that prophecy, even if it has definitively left the prophets, is perpetuated among the sages.[57] It can even maintain that the *halakha*, i.e., something along the lines of

---

55 Aristotle, *Politics*, II, 5, 1264a3.
56 Al-Farabi, *Kitâb al-Hurûf*, II, #143, ed. M. Mahdi (Beyrouth, Dâr al-Mashreq, 1962), pp. 151–2. On the passage, see my work *The Legend of the Middle Ages* (Chicago, The University of Chicago Press, 2009), p. 224.
57 Babylonian Talmud, treatises *Megillah*, II, 13, p. 19b, then *Baba Bathra*, I, 6, p. 12b.

"the path to follow," was so definitively granted to the sages, to men, that their agreement can correct the written revelation, even at the risk of formulations that verge on idolatry.[58]

Islam, too, appears to have had this same pang before the idea that revelation is ended.[59] It gave rise to several responses. Some have Mohammed say that, to be sure, prophecy is ended, but that there still remain "announcements" (*mubashshirât*). This enigmatic word was soon explained as signifying the "dreams" of Muslims (perhaps premonitory ones), which Mohammed said are part of prophecy. Other responses, which do not exclude the first, have another cycle, the cycle of holiness, follow that of prophecy. On its part, Shiism has a tendency to prolong prophecy by the transmission of "the light of Mohammed" in the line of imans, descendants of Ali. Hence its polemic with the majority-Sunni, which accuses it of deluting the exclusive character of prophecy, something that Shiism, as one can understand, denies.

As for Christianity, I will summarize its response, with all the risks this implies, in two points.

a) Everything is given, but everything is not manifested. The gift and the placing in evidence are two things. Here one has to reject the word-play of German idealists on *geoffenbart* ("revealed") and *offenbar* ("manifest"). Hegel gave it a great orchestration:

> Revealed religion (*geoffenbarte*) is thus the manifest religion (*offenbare*), since in it God has become totally

58 See the texts cited in J. Leibowitz, *Ha-'olam u-melo'o* (Jerusalem, Keter, 1987), pp. 99–101, and the commentaries by Leibowitz: "The Law says that what human intellect decides in the law is the divine law" (p. 100), and, above all, "oral law is of human making on the one hand; and on the other hand we receive it as a divine law – the very same law that we made by ourselves" (p. 99). Compare *Isaiah*, 2, 8.
59 See Y. Friedmann, *op. cit.*, pp. 199–205.

manifest (*offenbar*). . . . God no longer has any secrets (*Es ist nichts geheimes mehr an Gott*).[60]

I would respond: God gives himself entirely. But if he gives himself entirely, he gives himself as he is, thus as mysterious. His mysterious character owes to the fact that he is a personal being, and that every person, even a human person, even the person closest to us, we ourselves, is and remains an unfathomable mystery. To be sure, God "no longer has any secrets from us" (*John*, 15, 15). He does not retain anything that he refuses us, keeping it for himself. But he *is* a secret insofar as he is a person. It could even be the case that the gift and the secret, far from being mutually exclusive, grow together. One can employ the formulation of Dionysius the Areopagite:

> He is hidden even after his manifestion, or to use an even more divine formula, he is also hidden in his manifestation This aspect of Jesus is hidden, and the mystery attached to him is not removed by any discourse, or understanding. On the contrary, spoken, he remains non-said, understood, not-understood.[61]

Pascal echoed him a thousand years later:

> [God] has remained hidden under the veil of the nature that cloaked him from us until the Incarnation; and when it was necessary that he appeared, he hid himself even more by covering himself with humanity. He was much more recognizable when he was invisible than when he made himself visible.[62]

60 G. W. F. Hegel, *Philosophie der Religion, op. cit.*, p. 100. One finds the same word-play in Schelling, *Philosophie der Offenbarung*, lesson XXIV (Darmstadt, Wissenschaftliche Buchgesellschaft, [no date given]), p. 11 and XXV, p. 31.

61 Ps.-Denis the Areopagite, *Letter 3*, Patrologia Graeca, 3, 1069A; see the commentary on the passage by Maximus the Confessor, *Ambigua*, PG, 91, 1048D–1049B.

62 Pascal, 4th Letter to Mademoiselle de Roannez, around the 29th of

One sees the paradox: the retreat of the sacred does not come from the fact that it holds itself back by remaining in its transcendence, as is the case in the negative theologies sketched by the philosophers, especially neoplatonists. On the contrary, it flows from the fact that he has fully given himself: "it is by showing himself that God hides" (*phainomenos kruptetai*).

b) After the Son comes the Holy Spirit. The Spirit, as we have seen, adds nothing to what – or rather, to whom – has been said. He says nothing more than what the Son says – the Son who is himself his "message," not just delivering one. But the Spirit causes speech, he stirs up in human beings the word of response. This is what the *Epistle to the Romans* says: "The Spirit intercedes for us" (8, 26). The Spirit, though, limits himself to "inexpressible sighs," or to the infantine word "Abba" ("dad"), which is the result of the very first opposition of distinctive features, and the root of human language.[63] Everything else is the speech that we humans have to compose by our lives. He who has said everything, who has shown all his cards, gives the humans he addresses full liberty to respond. To be sure, he teaches man and, by that fact, frees him; as the jargon puts it, he "emancipates" him. The book of *Genesis* explains how God, having created and named the principal elements of the world (I, 5, 8, 10), allows Adam to give to the animals names that he agrees to learn from him (2, 19–20). In the same way, for Christianity, God, having said in Christ everything that he is, allows us the next word.

At bottom, what God has to say, and what he in fact says, in one sense is not a lot. He perhaps only says *one* thing. But it is the thing that he alone can say. In the Old Testament, it is his name (*Exodus*, 3, 14). The New Testament explains this same name by

October, 1656, in *Oeuvres Complètes*, ed. J. Mesnard, t. 3 (Paris, Desclée de Brouwer, 1991), p. 1035.
63 See R. Jakobson, "Why 'Mama' and 'Papa,'" in *Selected Writings*, I, "Phonological Studies," (La Haye and Paris, Mouton, 1971 [2nd ed.]), pp. 538–543.

agapè, "charity" (1 *John*, 4, 8). Man has as his task, to say the rest. And salvation is that he is made capable of doing so.

2. *The word now belongs to us*

Once God has said all that he has to say, and precisely because he has said everything, he gives the platform to man. What obliges man to take up the task of speaking, is not the silence that would be due to a simple and total absence, or to the disinterest of a God situated too high or too far away from him. It is the silence that comes from the fact that God has said everything he can say, to wit: everything he is. A silence of this quality is necessary for the human word to be truly authorized. Not merely permitted, even less simply tolerated, but endowed with the very authority of God, who in fact gives it.

This divine attitude is already prefigured in the writings of the Old Testament. The biblical God grants the word to his creature. Besides the passage I just cited, where God agrees to learn from man, one can cite the extraordinary scene in which Abraham bargains with God, who had shared his intention of destroying Sodom (*Genesis*, 18).[64]

Violence cannot be exorcised except when God himself agrees to enter into debate with men. One should read in this sense the passages of the prophets which are presented in the form of reproaches that God makes to men, a literary genre that exegetes call by the Hebrew word *rîv* ("contestation, indictment").[65] One could also speak of a "diatribe" in the original sense of the word, a contradictory discussion in which the orator appeals to the audience itself and brings it forward as a witness; or, again, one could speak of "improperia," according to the name that has become traditional in the liturgy of Holy Friday. The initial form of these no doubt first appeared in the second century, with Meliton of

---

64 On the exemplary value of this passage, see B. Saint-Sernin, *Le rationalisme qui vient*, *op. cit.*, pp. 61 & 165.

65 See the classical article by B. Gemser, "The Rib- or Controversy-Pattern in Hebrew Mentality," *Supplement to Vetus Testamentum*, 3, 1955, pp. 120–127.

Sardes, in a polemic in which Christians returned to Jews the critique that the Jews originally leveled against them.[66]

The prophets have God speak as if he brought an indictment against his people (*Hosea*, 4, 1–5; *Micah*, 6, 1–5; *Isaiah*, 3, 13–15). On the other hand, man dares to protest against God. Job is the most extended example. Psalm 22, which Jesus recited on the cross, is perhaps the most intense: it dares to ask God the question, why? and thus asks him to render an account. This is not a matter of a revolt, though: man, it has been said, appeals from God to the very concept of God.[67]

The two-part relationship between God and the people thus changes into a relation with three elements. God himself invokes a third who serves as a witness (*Isaiah*, 1, 2). *Deuteronomy* powerfully deploys this theme (4, 26; 30, 19; 32, 1). With the introduction of the third term, the entire dimension of the juridical appears, and with it one leaves the narrow domain in which master and slave encounter.[68]

One can draw a consequence from this that is very important for the violent or non-violent character of a religion. Most often, it is asked if the religion encourages violence among men. In fact, though, the question first of all concerns the very mode in which God reveals himself. The decisive question is first of all that of the character of the contact between God and men, whether God chooses to employ violence, or not, on men. The fact of violence depends in the final analysis on the fashion in which God chooses to present himself to them.

---

66 Meliton of Sardes, *Sur la Pâque*, #73–91, I. 534–679, ed. O. Perler (Paris, Le Cerf [*Sources chrétiennes*, n. 123]), pp. 10–12; see S. Pines, "From Darkness into Great Light" [with a complementary note by D. Flusser], in *Studies in the History of Religion* (*The Collected Works of S. P.*, t. 4) (Jerusalem, Magnes Press, 1996), pp. 3–10.

67 The formula is from R. Spaemann, "Die Frage nach der Bedeutung des Wortes 'Gott,'" in *Einsprüche. Christliche Reden* (Einsiedeln, Johannes, 1977), p. 26.

68 See A. Kojève, *Esquisse d'une phénoménologie du droit* (Paris, Gallimard, 1981), p. 23 and passim.

With the silence of God, one born of an entire Word already spoken, human agency finds itself liberated. It is no longer suspended in anticipation of what God could still have to say, or, what happens more often, what those who claim to speak in his name have to say.

John of the Cross underscores this:

> God is so much a friend [of the fact that] the government and management of man occurs by way of another man, one similar to him, and that it is by natural reason that man is ruled and governed, that he totally willed, for the things that He communicates to us in a supernatural way, that we would not give them entire credit, and that they would not have full force and certainty, until they passed by this human conduit which is the mouth of man.[69]

John employs an interesting expression: "God is 'friend' (*amigo*) of the fact that. . . ." He means to say by this, to be sure, that it is God's will, his design, his plan – however one might want to put it – that things occur in a certain way. But it is remarkable that he thus avoids the language of will and command, as well as of desire, for the sake of that of friendship. God's behavior is thus placed under its principle of intelligibility, what the Greek Fathers called the "friendship of God for man" (*philanthropia*).[70] The patristic concept of "philanthropy" itself translates the revolution introduced by the words of the Evangelist John puts in the mouth of Jesus, addressing himself to his disciples: "I no longer call you slaves (*doulos*). . . . I call you friends" (*John*, 15, 15).[71] In this optic, one can grasp the fundamental misconception of the Grand

69 John of the Cross, *SMC*, #9, p. 203.
70 On this concept, see H. Petré, Caritas, *Étude sur le vocabulaire latin de la charité chrétienne* (Louvain, Spicilegium Sacrum Lovaniense, 1948), pp. 207–11.
71 On this phrase, see the meditation by G. Vattimo, *Espérer croire*, trans. J. Rolland (Paris, Le Seuil, 1998), pp. 15, 47, 55, 85. This verse is the central theme of this little book.

Inquisitor in Dostoievski's great novel, *The Brothers Karamazov*. The old man who had captured the Christ, returned to earth in Seville at the height of the Inquisition, visits him in jail where he awaits the fire. He recalls for him a principle rather close to what his compatriot and contemporary John taught: "You do not have the right to add anything to what has already been said by you before. . . . Do you have the right to reveal anything to us, be it but one of the mysteries of the world from which you came?"[72] Here it is a matter of not putting at risk the highest principle that Jesus wanted to defend, man's capacity to freely give his faith. But we know that for the Inquisitor, "there has never been anything more intolerable for man and for society than liberty! . . . Inertia and even death are better for man than free will when it comes to the knowledge of good and evil."[73] He flatters himself with having relieved humanity of the burden of freedom.[74] To do so, however, he had to assume an awesome responsibility, a terrible suffering: having to lie with full knowledge of the truth, in order to allow the masses to live with consoling illusions.[75] At least partially in agreement with his brother Alyosha (as well as the personal views of the author), Ivan sees in the Grand Inquisitor the achieved type – if not the hyperbolic type – of the will to power ascribed to the Catholic Church, above all to the papacy and the Jesuits. Christ would have given the pope all authority, and was beseeched not to disturb it before the proper time.[76] To set Christ's silence against human liberty is the most radical perversion one could conceive, because this silence has precisely for its goal to

---

72 F. M. Dostoïevski, *The Brothers Karamazov*, II, v, 5 (Moscow, Transitkniga, 2006), pp. 254–55.

73 *Ibid.*, p. 256, then 258–59.

74 Here I reprise a phrase, perhaps too perfect to be true, that H. Rauschning put in the mouth of Hitler. H. Rauschning, *Gespräche mit Hitler* (Vienne, Europaverlag, 1973 [Zurich, 1940]), xv, p. 212.

75 F. M. Dostoïevski, *op. cit.*, pp. 258, 263.

76 *Ibid.*, p. 255 (Ivan), 264 (Alyosha). Ivan's affirmation probably alludes to the analogous request of the demons to Christ (Matthew, 8, 29).

allow man to speak and to permit him to respond in full knowledge to what is offered him.

3. A general rule

It is precisely such a way of leaving room for man that is expressed by a general rule of how God conducts himself toward man:

> Ordinarily, everything that can be done by the care (*industria*) and reflection (*consejo*) of men, He [God] neither does it nor says it . . . [God approved the counsel of Jethro to Moses] when He had not given any himself, because it was a matter of something that could depend upon the capacity (*caber en*) of human reason and judgment.[77]

It is striking to recall that the example chosen here by John, i.e., the counsel given to Moses by his father-in-law, is at it were the reflected image of the policy adopted according to him by God himself. Moses was counseled to delegate the authority to judge conflicts of a "civil" nature that could arise among the children of Israel, in order to leave Moses the time to devote himself to his mission as a prophet.

One point merits being forcefully underlined. What John expresses here is, at bottom, nothing other than what would be much later formulated under the technical name of "the principle of subsidiarity."[78] By this, one means the rule according to which a higher authority does not have the right to intervene in what an inferior level can, by itself, properly effect; this has the corollary that the superior has the duty to aid the inferior when it cannot operate successfully on its own. The domain of application of this principle most often is that of politics: what the family can do well by itself, the education of children, for example, civil society ought not take in hand; what civil society is capable of doing, for example, producing wealth, the State ought not to mix itself with,

---

77 *SMC*, #13, p. 205.
78 See Chantal Millon-Delsol, *Le Principe de subsidiarité* (Paris, PUF, coll. "Que sais-je?," n. 2793, 1993).

except where the laws of the market left to themselves would leave some citizens in a situation where they would lose their ability to use their civic rights.

More recently, this principle has become popular in connection with the construction of the European Union: what the national States suffice to do well, European institutions ought not to run. In this connection, it has been recalled that the oldest formulation of the principle of subsidiarity had as its context Pope Pius XI recalling a tenet of the social doctrine of the Church. He opposed to a principle that Italian fascism itself called "totalitarian," the right of parents to refuse the "martialization" of their children. Both this reminder and this justification were perfectly correct. But they did not go to the bottom of things, by failing to show that the social doctrine of the Church itself derives its principles – at least the one we are talking about now – from the highest regions of theology.

Now, this is precisely what the text of John of the Cross enables us to see. A rule like this one, for which the principle of subsidiarity constitutes an application in a particular domain, is nothing less than the one that governs the relations of God toward his creation. This, according to St. Thomas, is the doctrine of Providence: God gives to each creation everything it needs to attain its proper good, but he allows it to choose for itself the ways and means that will allow it to attain its good.[79]

Conclusion

That God chose not to "parachute in" what he had to say, but to begin by expressing himself in a history, a liberating history, was already a preparation for the Incarnation. By it, the divine Word became flesh, that is, immersed himself in what by definition is mute. With the death of Christ, God said all he had to say. In this

---

79 St. Thomas, *Summa contra Gentiles*, III, #111 ff. I hope to develop this teaching in a later work.

way, the way in which the God of Christians speaks does not result in the silence of men. The divine word does not replace the human word, it does not eclipse it, it does not dictate in advance what it must repeat. On the contrary, it gives rise to it as the response it awaits.

Chapter 6
A God Who Asks Nothing of Us

A God who leaves us free must also be a God that asks nothing of us. The late Polish philosopher Leszek Kolakowski entitled a book on Pascal *God Owes Us Nothing*.[1] In homage to his thought, I would like to develop the idea that we owe nothing to God, either, because, if it is true that he *gives* us everything, he *asks* nothing of us. In particular, he does not ask us to conduct ourselves in this-or-that manner.

Why do this here? Because we are still too often persuaded that religion is a kind of morality, or at least an adjunct and aid to it. In the countries where there are religious courses in the public school curricula, in Belgium or Germany, the children of parents who do not want their children to take them are given "secular morals." If this can replace religion, this implies that religion is a kind of morality. People believe that Christianity is a moral code. Instead of citing contemporary twits, let us cite the fictional archetype, Monsieur Homais in *Madame Bovary*, who believes that Christianity "introduced into the world a morality."[2] As a corollary to this, and in the other direction, some believe they have made a great discovery when they declare that there can be morality without religion.

I. I know what to do

1. *The amplitude of the normative*
In order to take the measure of the question of morality, one has

1 L. Kolakowski, *God Owes Us Nothing: A Brief Remark on Pascal's Religion and the Spirit of Jansenism* (Chicago, The University of Chicago Press, 1995).
2 G. Flaubert, *Madame Bovary*, III, 9 (Paris, Nelson), p. 453.

to step back and take in the domain of norms as a whole. Essentially, it coincides with the domain of culture. The basic question for this is: "What ought I to do?" How ought I to act, to act well? To be sure, this is true first of all for morality; Kant summarized its central question in the preceding question.[3] But this is true for *everything* that we do. To speak with Aristotle, this is true for the entire domain of "practical philosophy." This begins with the self-government of the individual, i.e., ethics. But then it encompasses the relations between spouses, between parents and children, and masters and subordinates (what the Ancients called "economics"). In the third place, it comprehends the domain of politics and law. Finally, this is also true of the domain of what we *make* or fabricate, what Aristotle called "poetics": an object has to be fashioned, maintained or repaired, the services of the plumber or the piano-tuner have to be provided, as contracts stipulate, "according to the rules of the art."

Contemporary anthropology says the same thing in a more refined and general way. It notes that there is no culture without the rules of language, without rules of marriage and affiliation (what is put negatively as the prohibition of incest); there are even rules for cooking. Grammar, getting-along, and so forth – all this regulated behavior indicates that one has to conduct oneself in a certain way or face penalties, whose gravity goes from ridicule to social ostracism, with raised eyebrows somewhere there.

One can very well attempt to attach all or some of these norms (and some have tried) to a divine origin.[4] Ancient Greece and Israel both did, each in its own way. Israel developed a very sophisticated normative system, with very precise rituals. Already, the Pentateuch contained detailed commandments. The successive meditation of the rabbis, first collected in the Talmud (the Mishna around 200 C.E., then the Gemara around 500 C.E.), and continued to our day, has elaborated a system of norms, the

3   E. Kant, *Kritik der reinen Vernunft*, A 804–805, B 832–833.
4   See my work *The Law of God, op. cit.*

halakha, which, at least in principle, ought to stipulate exactly the status of every action.

2. *What does God ask?*

However, one also finds in the Bible texts that suggest that what one must do to satisfy what God requires does not require any explanation. After having retraced the stages of the history of the people of Israel from the exit from Egypt, *Deuteronomy* has Moses say: "And now, Israel, who does Yahweh your God require (*sho'el*) of you?" (*Deuteronomy*, 10, 12). The classic Jewish commentatory of the eleventh century, Rashi, explains the question: Yahweh asks nothing as expiation for the sins of Israel that Moses had just listed (in a sort of general confession).[5] The answer that follows begins with vague formulas ("love Yahweh"), then is attached rather awkwardly, and in a circular manner, to the concrete dispositions promulgated in the book itself.

One reads in the prophet Micah: "He/It has made you know, o man, what is good, what Yahweh demands (*doresh*) of you: nothing other than to accomplish justice (*mishpat*), to love with tenderness (*ahavat hèsèd*), and to walk humbly (*hatsnea' lekhet*) with your God" (6, 8). In the context, it is a matter of relativizing, if not totally rejecting, the bloody sacrifices. Who, or what, the undesignated subject is in Hebrew, the commentators discussed. Would it be the previous prophets whose teaching would be summed up in one key word or another: justice in Amos, love in Hosea, humility in Isaiah? That is certainly possible. But what they demanded was nothing that was not already known, nothing but the "grand platitudes" C. S. Lewis wrote about. Therefore, they are only expressed in the vaguest of manners. It is not said *how* to accomplish justice, *how* to love with tenderness, *how* to walk with humility. In other words, God does not furnish a civil code, a morality, nor a method of spirituality.

Does this mean that law, morality, all the rules, are useless? Or worse, that one can replace them with vague sentiments? The

5   Rashi *ad loc.*, in *Miqra'ot gedolot* (Jerusalem, Eshkol, 1976), p. 32b.

temptation to do so is not absent from Christianity, and Christians have sometimes succumbed, even from the time of the New Testament. It was against such back-slidings that St. Paul had to recall that, "if everything is permitted, not everything makes a positive contribution (*sumpherei*), not everything edifies (*oikodomei*)" (1 *Corinthians*, 10, 23; cf. 6, 12). Those who succumbed to these temptations won't complain when they are accused of "lawlessness" (*anomia*). In truth, we have great need of being clear about law and morality, the greatest need. But, *in principle* we have in ourselves what is needed to satisfy the need, without having to get our cue from a divine prompter. It behooves man to find the ways in which to regulate his personal life and the community. This is a difficult task, one that always has to be resumed anew, but it is one for which the strength of human intellect has to suffice.

This was not an invention of Paul. The same thing is implied in Jesus's message. All his sayings suppose that the rules to follow are known: "convert . . . ," that is, "turn in the direction you already know"; "you will be judged" – according to criteria you already know; "God will pardon your sins" – which transgress a law you already know. Jesus did not preach morality. He announced forgiveness. He did not need to say what needed to be done: the Law was known, it was Moses's law. Paul, when turning toward the pagans, enlarged things by borrowing the notion of conscience from stoicism. The noble pagans had the Law written in their heart, they were "a law unto themselves" (*Romans*, 2, 14). The Greek phrase sketches what will become the word "autonomy."

Christianity has remained faithful to this principle. We possess within ourselves what is necessary to know the rules to follow. To be sure, a nuance is needed. It is quite obvious that this does not mean that we will *always* have an *explicit* awareness of what we should do. Our moral conscience passes through social life, without which we would not acquire language. Both society and language convey a thousand habits that have become self-evident. Moreover, we can forget, we can also decide to forget, and act in bad faith. Our conscience can become darkened for reasons owing

to our personal or collective past, our past or present surround-
ings, in short, a thousand causes. We, moreover, can find ourselves
before objectively complex and perplexing situations (for example, many of today's bioethical dilemmas). In them it is difficult to
grasp the good. But the essential remains: we do have the individual and collective instruments that allow us to know what to do.

3. The end of the law

What, then, is the problem? Let us begin with the sighs of St. Paul,
who declares that "to want [the good] is in my power (*parakeitai*),
to accomplish it is not"; "it is not what I want that I do, it is what
I hate that I do"; "the good that I desire, I do not do it, but the
evil that I do not want, I do it" (*Romans*, 7, 18; 15, 19). These
formulations are pregnant with a revolution.

Previously, people had taken the measure of the amplitude of
the normative. Paul's formulations sweep it away, or rather, rele-
gate it to the inessential. The problem is not to know what to do.
One could even dare to say: Kant's second question ("What ought
I to do?") is a foolish question. (As a matter of fact, Kant himself
said that it was not as if he was telling us what one ought to do,
as if we didn't know.) We desire or will the good, says Paul; this
implies that we already know where to seek it. The real problem
is to know why, when we already know what we ought to do – in
fact, we know all too well – the real problem is: why we still do
not do it.

The problem ranges in two directions, each of which corresponds to a dimension of time, the past and the future. The first is
to know how we can receive forgiveness for our past sins: the
answer is mercy. The second is to know how we can receive yet
again the ability to do the good: the answer is grace. Thus, Christian
revelation is not the revelation of a Law but of mercy and grace. In
this way, too, Christianity opens a sort of space for freedom. It is up
to the human to whom they are given to find how to "cash out" the
good, to define appropriately his self-government, more prosaically,
how to wash and clothe himself, to live intelligently with his
spouse, his children, his superiors and inferiors, how to work and

how to enjoy his leisure. God has no need to furnish man with a manual directing him at each step. These were not invented by Christianity, in fact they were invented by no one. In this connection, one could use a phrase of Chesterton taken out of context: "Catholic doctrine and discipline may be walls; but they are the walls of a playground."[6] In order to find good ways of playing in the sandbox, one needs imagination. The basic principle of Christianity is, therefore, "imagination in authority."

I said at the beginning that God does not ask us to conduct ourselves in a rigidly determined manner. This does not mean that conduct is a matter of indifference. What might be thought to lead to libertinage in fact places us before a somewhat terrifying responsibility. Each way of behaving contains an internal logic that, in the final analysis, causes it to lead necessarily either to life or to death. To be sure, this transpires by way of more or less complex mediations, which produce their effects at the end of more, or less, long delays.

Now, we are not aware at the outset of the immanent logic of our practices. That is why we have need not only of moral rules, but of a moral *life*. And this implies constant attention to the circumstances of the action, an effort to refine our moral sensibility, and permanent contact with those ohers, contemporaries or belonging to the past, friends or bed-side reading, who can share with us their experience in these matters.

II. God's expectation

1. The vegetal model

How, then, can we express the bond of a creature with a God who demands nothing of it? In the Bible, the rapport between God and the creature who recapitulates within himself all of creation (I am speaking, of course, of man) is expressed by, of all things, a vegetal image. First of all, in the case of the people of Israel, God

6   G. K. Chesterton, *Orthodoxy*, chap. 9 (San Francisco, Ignatius Press, 1995 [1908]), p. 152.

plants a vine. The image was probably invented by Hosea (10, 1) but it was Isaiah who gave it all of its dimensions by making it the subject of a parable: "My beloved had a vineyard on a very fertile hill. He digged it and cleared it of stones, and planted it with choice vines; he built a watchtower in the midst of it, and hewed out a wine vat in it; and he looked for it to yield grapes, but it yielded wild grapes" (5, 1–2). God, thus, is likened to a vinekeeper who began by planting a vine. The comparison is quite apt, because it encapsulates the way in which Israel understood its own history, that of an originally nomadic people who settled down.

What happened next in the parable does not concern us here. I only retain the image, which recurs henceforth throughout the Old Testament. It is repeated quite self-consciously in several of Jesus's parables, where he reflects upon his mission. This is the case of the parable of the sower, found in the three synoptic Gospels (e.g., *Matthew*, 13, 1–9), and above all in that of the homicidal tenants (*Matthew*, 21, 33–43 and parallels), as well as in the parable of the vine and the branches in *St. John* (15, 1–8). The image received a powerful development when the Fathers of the Church took up the stoic idea of "seminal reasons": creation is the deed by which God sows seeds that will develop, each in its own time.[7] In the famous (and untranslatable) Latin palindrome: ROTAS OPERA TENET AREPO SATOR, "The Sower (*Sator*)" probably signifies the Christian God.

This image helps us to formulate a fundamental distinction between "ask" and "expect" or "await." One asks, much less demands, nothing from a plant. In fact, one cannot ask anything of it. One waits for it to grow, and one expects it to grow if one has taken the requisite measures. The vinekeeper "hopes" (*qawweh*) that his vine will give grapes (*Isaiah*, 5, 2b. 4b.); in the same way, God expects from his people justice (5, 7b). To be sure, it often happens that God is represented as addressing his people,

7   See, for example, St. Augustine, *De Genesi ad litteram*, IX, 18, 33, ed. J. Zycha, CSEL, 28–1 (Vienna, Tempsky, 1894), pp. 132–33, PL, 34, 406 [d].

even reproaching it for its infidelity. But is this a way of asking it for something, much less demanding it? Even there where God is addressing himself to a being capable of understanding and, therefore, that he can ask it something, this request is nothing other than a way of reminding it of what he expects.

God expects nothing more than to see his creatures deploy themselves according to their immanent logic. When it is a plant, to grow, to seek nourishment and its sexual partner when an animal. In the case of man, a being with several levels, one must consider several planes: what is expected of him as a living being, is to put in place the conditions of his continued existence. As a being endowed with language and everything implied by its possession, he must organize a social and political life, and a moral life. Nothing more enters in except the immanent logic of what he is.

I underscore the term "immanent." In order to elucidate it, it is helpful to have recourse to an old word, that of "nature." What causes the vine to produce grapes is what we ordinarily call "nature." We can understand the word as designating a power of growth that traverses the entirety of the living (Nature), or what a thing is at its core, in which case we speak of "the nature of" the thing, in our case: the nature of the vine, which is to produce grapes and not bananas. The Old Testament did not know the word "nature" (nor, for that matter, did it have any philosophical concepts). But it contains some of its concepts in the stories it tells. The first narrative of creation insists upon the "natural" aspect of things in a rather freighted passage: "The earth produced vegetation: the plants bearing seed according to their species (*mîn*), trees, according to their species, producing fruit containing their seeds" (*Genesis*, 1, 12).

God expects, and awaits, that things and events will bear their fruit. Here I will give two examples, borrowed from each of the two testaments that form the Christian Bible.

2. The Old Testament

According to the first creation-narrative, God gave names to some of the things that he created. Thus, he named in succession a pair of opposites: day and night (1, 5); then a single reality, the heaven (1, 8); finally, another pair of opposites, the earth and the seas (1, 10). These namings took place, respectively, the first, second, and third day. During the three following days, God did not name anything. The fourth day in fact is something of an 'avoiding-a-name'. Recounting the way in which God made the two major heavenly bodies, the sacred author takes care not to call them by their name of Sun and Moon; he employs the name of an instrument that we translate by "luminaries" (i.e., "lamps").

Five realities in all, therefore, receive names from God. The sacred author who recounts this naming of creatures also has to say to what God gave a name: he, in his turn, must therefore name. God names the light "day" and the darkness "night." He names the firmament (*raqia'*) "heaven." He names the dry "earth" and the brought-together waters "seas" (in the plural). The first two realities are designated by names that come not only from the current lexicon but from immediate experience. But for the third, reasoning is required: it does not go without saying that the blue of the sky, or the stars, are fixed in a "firmament." One has to reflect, starting with the observation that the stars do not change place vis-à-vis each other; they move together in a bloc. Everything, that is, occurs as if they were supported by something solid, something firm – hence our word "firmament." For the last two realities, the writer, first of all, had to turn an adjective into a substantive ("the dry"), then construct a labored paraphrase. The realities thus designated by God are juxtaposed in an interesting way: the heaven and the earth do not oppose one another like the high and the low. The opposition is not vertical but horizontal, occurring between the emerged earth and the seas.

What meaning should be given to God's naming? In the case of the "heavens," one can follow the classical Jewish commentators, such as Rashi, and see in them an etymology according to which God would know the truth about the celestial vault that retains the waters above: the heavens, "the high" (*shamayim*) is "the water" (*sham mayim*).

According to the second creation-narrative, God brought all the animals to Adam to see if he would choose from among them a partner – without success, so that God drew Eve from Adam's side. "YHWH formed from the earth all the beasts of the field and all the birds of the skies and led them to Man to see (*li-r'ot*) how he would call them (*mâ yiqra'lô*). And every living soul that Man named, that was its name" (2, 19). In the same way, once Man had declared himself dissatisfied with all the animals and God had had to draw a partner for him, not from the soil but his own flesh, it was still Man who called Eve "woman."

In so doing, God awaited man to name the animals and he thus agreed to learn something from his creature. By being silent and awaiting an answer, he created the first condition for a dialogue with man, which is to accept him as a partner who has something to say, something that is proper to him. Here one has a prefiguration of a movement of "retreat" by God that Isaac Luria, the principal representative of the kabbalistic school of Safed will later name *tsimtsum*.[8] Earlier St. Paul had seen in it the way in which Christ "emptied" himself (*kenôsis*) of the rank that equaled him to God (*Philippians*, 2, 7).

Among other things, to name is more than to lay out markers, it is to introduce the dimension of meaning. The name we give to things renders them accessible to us, and reveals what we wish to do with them. The biblical scene therefore suggests that the meaning of created realities is the work of man. It is interesting to observe that the corresponding scene in the Quran recounts, in contrast, how God taught men the names of things, a knowledge he refused to the angels (*Quran*, II, 31). God, far from having to learn from man the meaning that he would give to things, is the one who already possesses it. On his side, man no longer has to give meaning; it is enough to receive it from God. Meaning is not something to acquire; it is already received.

8 See G. Scholem, "Schöpfung aus Nichts und Selbstverschrankung Gottes," in *Über einige Grundbegriffe des Judentums* (Frankfort, Suhrkamp, 1970), pp. 53–89.

3. The New Testament

In the New Testament, one can cite the opening benediction of the *Letter to the Ephesians*: "Blessed be the God and Father of our Lord Jesus Christ, who has blessed us with all sorts of spiritual benedictions in the heavens, in Christ. He chose us in him from before the creation of the world, to be holy and immaculate in his presence, in love, determining in advance that we would be his adoptive sons in Jesus Christ" (1, 3–5).[9] The project of salvation as adoption by God is proposed to man. It encompasses "all things" that are to be recapitulated in Christ (1, 10). Such a plan implies the greatest possible universality.

But if the gift of God is antehistorical, the response of man is not. On the contrary, it is given in history. In a sense, this response is nothing but history itself, which what is proposed "in the heavens" makes possible. Man remains free to respond. His positive response is awaited and expected but it is not automatically given, in other words, it includes the risk of a "no." In this way, the time of history is not only the distance that separates man from his proper accomplishment. It is also the time of God's expectation (in the subjective genitive), the time in which God awaits man's response. There is something like a hope on God's part that precedes that of man. For Christianity, universalization is a historical movement. But this movement responds to a divine plan. And the realization of this plan is entrusted to human liberty. Human liberty receive from God only what it needs to be fully itself.

Here, too, a comparison with Islam is instructive. The Quran recounts a scene before the creation of the world, in which a "pact" (*mîthâq*) is made by which humanity is bound to God. All the generations to come are miraculously drawn from the loins of Adam and invited, as an ensemble, to attest to the lordship of the creator. This they do unanimously. The answer is given before history. In this way, humanity "witnesses against itself" (VII, 172).

9   See the commentary of H. Schlier, *Der Brief an die Epheser. Ein Kommentar*, Düsseldorf, Patmos, 1958, pp. 44–53.

Islam supposes that man is "naturally" muslim. According to an often cited *hadith*, "no new-born is born, if not according to nature (*fitra*). Then his two parents make him a Jew, a Christian, or a Zoroastrian."[10] There is no need for his parents to make him a Muslim: man is born a Muslim, it is his parents who make him a member of the other religions. A concrete application of this idea is found in Islamic law, where an infant that is found is deemed to be a Muslim until it is claimed by its parents.

As for the way in which Islam considers itself, two consequences follow: 1) No religion preceded Islam, which is the religion of Abraham, of Noah, and even of Adam. Islam, therefore, has inherited nothing and owes nothing to anyone. 2) An unbeliever is less blind or wicked than a kind of traitor toward everlasting fidelity; in the final analysis, a non-Muslim is, objectively speaking, an apostate. Similarly, the holy books of the other religions (the Torah, the Gospel) are not the prefigurations of the Quran, but on the contrary, they are distorted versions of an original message that essentially coincides with it.

III. Responding to the expectation

1. To eat

What, then, is the relation of man to this God who asks nothing of him? How can what God awaits from him happen? Here, I can appeal to a sentence of Walker Percy: "Jews wait for the Lord. Protestants sing hymns to him. Catholics say mass and eat him."[11] The passage is from a novelist, and is put in the mouth of a character who is not a theologian and who claims he is only uttering a commonplace. A theologian would not accept it as it is, or would parse it with long explanations. And he would be right to

10 *Hadith*, in A. J. Wensinck, *Condordance des traditions musulmanes* (Leyde, Brill), t. 5, p. 179b and elsewhere

11 W. Percy, *Love in the Ruins. The Adventures of a Bad Catholic at a Time Near the End of the World* (New York, Avon, 1978 [1971]), pp. 372–73.

do so. Nonetheless, it contains a profound truth, which goes beyond the Eucharist.

An entire aspect of the good is defined by the model of eating. The meaning of the word "good" does not allow itself to be rigorously defined.[12] But, at least for characterizing it, the most profound way to do so might be to start with the most banal meaning of the term, one that involves the sense of taste, which makes us say that a dish is "good." This, of course, is quite different from the famous phrase, "Bonum diffisivum sui," "The good tends to diffuse itself," a formulation of St. Bonaventure, inspired by the neoplatonism that was popular at the time.[13] It is a fine formulation, but one that we too often reduce to a rather abstract meaning. If we wish to retain the solar image implicit in it that we have received from Plato, it is time to take photosynthesis seriously. Or better: to think about the way in which animals are nourished. The good *nourishes*. To be sure, there are those who resist this suggestion. "The truth is not edible," wrote Celine somewhere.[14] And Victor Hugo became indignant at the idea of an "edible God."[15] On the other hand, the Bible has a passage that clearly implies that the relationship to the good, if this good is God, is one of eating: "Taste (*ta'amû*) and see how good is the Lord" (*Psalm*, 34, 9).

A God who allows himself to be eaten is a God who asks

---

12 G. E. R. Moore, *Principia Ethica* [1902], ed. revised by T. Baldwin (Cambridge, Cambridge University Press, 1993), I, #6–13, pp. 58–69.

13 See, for the Latin scholastics, Bonaventure, *Itinerarium mentis ad Deum*, VI, 2; St. Thomas, *Summa contra Gentiles*, I, 37; *De potentia*, q. 7, a. 5, ad7; for Jewish philosophy, Crescas, *Lumière du Seigneur*, II, 6, 5; ed. S. Fisher (Jerusalem, Sifrey Ramot, 1990), p. 271.

14 L.-F. Céline, *Voyage au bout de la nuit* (Paris, Gallimard, "Foliio," 1981), p. 461.

15 Cited without reference in P. Muray, *Le XIXe siècle à travers les âges*, *op. cit.*, p. 567. Muray rightly observes: "Ignorant, profoundly uneducated in theology, he [Hugo] ascribed to those who established [the religions] his own intentions."

nothing in exchange, not even that one love him. Or only in the sense that one "loves" a dish that one has found good, which one cannot know without eating it. In this connection, Nietzsche uttered an enormous falsehood. He grew indignant at the representation – a Christian one, he believed – of God that he found "too oriental": "How? A God who loves men, on the condition (*vorausgesetzt*) that they believe in him. . . !"[16] But how can one say that God gives himself under certain "conditions"? This is but a manner of speaking. The sole "condition" is that we accept what he gives us. But is this a "condition"? I can say: "The pharmacist fills my prescription, on the condition that I pay him." I can also say, if I wish: "The medicine cures me, on the condition that I take it." But this last formulation is strange. Who does not see that the meaning of "condition" is different in the two cases? It is obvious that medicine cures only if one takes it, while food only nourishes the one who eats it. It is only insofar as one does eat or take them that medicine and food actualize themselves as medicine and food. A baguette in the basket, aspirin in the medicine cabinet, are only food and medicine *in potentia*.

2. Faith

This God, is he such that one must believe in him? This is as foolish a question as to ask if this food will nourish me without eating it. To believe is not to pay God for a service that he provides me, it is to accept the service. It is to connect with God. Faith is the access to God, as vision is the access to colors, imagination, the access to images, and reason, the access to the calculable. God is such that he cannot be attained except by, and in, faith. To believe is to recognize oneself as needy and, by the same token, to receive what one needs. In faith, as with the proverbial "proof in the pudding," to believe is actually "to sit down to eat" and "to eat the meal." The economy of salvation is the arrangement that allows this to happen. It is not an obstacle between God and us.

16 F. Nietzsche, *Die Fröhliche Wissenschaft*, III, #141; KSA, t. 3, p. 489; see, too, *Also sprach Zarathustra*, IV, 6, KSA, t. 4, p. 324.

Quite the contrary, it is the very way in which God makes himself available as savior. If I fall into the water and someone throws me a lifeline, am I going to say: "This isn't the one I want! I demand that you save me with another means!"?

We hear it said that "faith is a gift of God." Nothing is more true, even more banally true. Pascal uses the phrase.[17] But most of the time this formula is used by unbelievers. And they quote it in order to excuse themselves for not "having" faith. It can even be the case that they use it, more or less consciously, to accuse God for not having given faith to them, for having refused it to them while he gave this privilege to others who, perhaps, deserve it less than they do.

In truth, the formula is not correct unless two conditions are met. On one hand, faith is not the only gift of God, it is only one of the gifts of God; in the final analysis, God gives everything that is. On the other hand, and as a consequence: precisely because God gives to every creature, he gives to each according to what it is, its "nature," as we saw. Thus, he gives to the inanimate according to the manner of the inanimate, to the plant and animal as plants and animals, and so forth. To man, God gives as one gives to man. Now, faith is not a gift of God in general, but a gift of God to man. That is, it is a gift that is addressed to man as man, in his properly human dimension, not what belongs to him as merely organic or sentient. The gift of the faith, therefore, has nothing to do with the qualities that, even though they are present in man, are not, properly speaking, human. This is the case with the color of his hair or his skin, which are vegetal features. Nor is it the case with pleasure and pain, which also concern living being in general, including animals. This extends to human happiness or misery, to the extent that they depend upon chance or misfortune. It is also true of a certain "intelligence," a pure capacity to calculate, which can belong to computers. The faith is a gift in the measure that it is proposed to that alone which makes man what – or who – he is: liberty.

The sole appropriate subject of faith is liberty. What, then, is its

17 Pascal, *Pensées*, #279, op. cit., t. 2, p. 202; see also #248, p. 181.

object? The question of the object of faith has been posed, and some have wanted to substitute for faith in God, faith in man, that is, confidence in his moral capacities, despite all the facts that witness to his perversity. This noble idea appeared in a particularly grand way in Fichte.[18] It has been rather trivilialized in the subsequent rhetoric of secular humanists. In truth, however, if one places oneself in the perspective I am attempting to delineate here, the alternative between the two objects of faith loses its oppositional character. The idea of "faith in man," of a faith that would have man for its object, is fundamentally sound. But the question remains, who can be the subject of this faith, who is capable of exercising such a faith? Who, in short, can believe in man? Man himself? But "to believe in oneself" is the very definition of madness.[19] Only God can "believe in man." And this is exactly what he does.

In this way, what is called "faith in God" by man is a response to God's faith in man, that is, in the initial confidence (*fides*) that God bestowed on the human creature. By faith, we agree to "plug into" God and share his faith.

3. Pride and humility

From this, one can understand the reason why the root of sin is *superbia*. In order to better understand the word, which we normally translate as "pride," let us take an etymological detour. The underlying image, one derived from agriculture, is expressive: it goes back to the indo-european root *bhu-, which appears also in the Greek *phyomai*, which a Greek ear would hear (perhaps mistakenly) in the word *physis*, which we translate as "nature."[20] In Latin, a language of market-gardeners, it yields

18 J. G. Fichte, *Anweisung zum seligen Leben*, 10th lesson, in *Ausgewählte Werke*, ed. F. Medicus (Darmstadt, Wissenschaftliche Buchgessellschaft, 1962), t. 3, p. 161.
19 G. K. Chesterton, *Orthodoxy, op. cit.*, chap. 2, pp. 18–19. In a wholly different context, Sartre writes: "one cannot admit that a man can level a judgment on man" (*L'existentialisme est un humanisme* (Paris, Nagel, 1970), p. 90–92).
20 Aristotle, *Metaphysics*, V, 4, 1014b16–17.

pro-bus, *super-bus*: the honest man (*probus*) is he whose stem grows straight, while the proud man (*superbus*) is he who grows too tall. The meaning of the second word probably refers to the one who seeks to overtop others, e.g., in the famous history of Tarquinius, the king of Rome, who was surnamed "the Proud." He mowed down the poppies that stood out in a field, thus indicating to his son that he had to execute the notables of a conquered town.

Christianity, perhaps more profoundly, understands that the real danger lies not in growing too much, in developing excessively. In fact, the danger is quite the contrary. The goal sought by growth, as the fourth evangelist has Jesus say in the parable of the vine, is "to bear much fruit" (*John*, 15, 2, 8). Pride consists in forgetting these nourishing roots, and far from leading to an exaggerated growth, it leads to withering.

The contrary of pride, and the medicine which heals it, is humility.[21] Humility, as its Latin etymology indicates – which will continue to be seen throughout the Middle Ages – is that by which I remain close to the nourishing *humus*, i.e., soil.[22] This is why Christian humility, far from being the contrary of "pagan" magnanimity, is what makes it possible. To remain close to the root that gives life has no other goal but to "render" or return what one has received. God has no need of anything and does not ask us for anything when he gives. The goal is to continue to receive and not to dry and wither, severed from the root.

This is why – contrary to what is often imagined – humility has nothing to do with pusillanimity. This is the vice by which I judge that I am incapable of the great things that, in truth, I am capable of.[23] The New Testament provides a magnificent example

21 St. Augustine, *City of God*, XIV, xiii, 1, Patrologia Latina, 41, 421 [b], BA, t. 35, p. 412.
22 See, for example, Isidore, *Etymologies*, X, 116; PL, 82, 379b, and also Meister Eckhart, *Expositio Libri Exodi* [on 20, 24], ed. K. Weib, in *Lateinische Werke* (Stuttgart, Kohlhammer, 1992), t. 2, #242, p. 198.
23 Aristotle, *Nicomachean Ethics*, IV, 3, 1123b9–11, 1125a17–23.

of pusillanimity in the parable of the talents and the third servant, who buried the money that the master has given him. It is interesting to note that the character did not understand the master who *gave* him of his substance, nor that he needed to make it his own. He had a false image of the master, whom he mistook as hard and demanding. Concerning the other two servants, it is not said that they *returned* what had been given to them and that they made to multiply. On the contrary, having shown themselves capable of receiving, they received even more.[24]

Now, one can understand why Augustine said that "obedience is the mother of the virtues."[25] The virtues are different ways of that the good is refracted, that liberty can make the good its own, which is, precisely, by "doing" it. Now, what does obedience mean here? It is not at all a matter of submitting to an authority that seeks its own interest; it is a matter of adhering to the Good, to the one who wishes me good. According to a text that Augustine often cites (and which I have already spoken of)[26]: "It is good for me to adhere to God" (*Mihi adhaerere* [in Hebrew, *qirba*, in Greek, *proskollasthai*] *Deo bonum est*" (*Ps.* 72, 28). The relation to the good is not complete in submission, it ends with identification, in keeping with the old idea of the divinization (*theôsis*) of man, as developed by the Greek Fathers of the Church.

4. Sacrifice

To adhere to God? To be sure, but which one? "The good Lord," as we say. But precisely! How to know which one is good? How to identify the true God and distinguish him from his rivals? All believers claim to adore true gods. At the extreme, they claim that all the gods of others are false, they are no more than "idols." In this way, one imagines a line of contending divinities – in order to

---

24 *Matthew*, 25, 14–30. Here I recall a fascinating interpretation of this parable give by Marie Balmary. I do not know if she has published it.

25 St. Augustine, , XIV, xii, PL, 41, 420 [bc], BA, t. 35, p. 408.

26 St. Augustine, *ibid.*, X, vi; xviii; XII, ix.

send them all away.[27] In truth, the question is not, as once again the imbeciles would have us believe, to know how the true God is called, or how many there are. The name or the number of gods, these are questions for naïfs. Let us, in contrast, apply our criterion: the true God does not demand anything, he only gives. A false god, on the contrary, only demands.

In the *City of God*, Augustine conducts a critique of what we call "paganism" and in this context sketches a genealogy of what we would call religiosity. This consists, he says in a lapidary phrase, in "making the false gods that one wants" (*fecit sibi quos voluit* [. . .] *falsos deos*). In the first place, Augustine shows – in order to denounce it – the arbitrary character of these gods, the interminable list of which he is pleased to detail. In contrast to the true God, whom one could call the "natural" god, these gods are artificial or factitious. (The corresponding Portuguese adjective, *feitiço*, is the root of the word "fetish.") It seems to me, however, that we can and must go deeper, and understand that these "gods" are not merely the product of a will that would have chosen to make them this-or-that, but that they are the way in which the will manifests, in an objective fashion, what it wills or desires.

These gods are demanding. As a character in a play by Aristophanes observes in a sarcastic tone, their statutes represent them with their hand outstretched, not to give but to receive.[28] Moreover, the fact that these gods are mendicants is not one attribute among many: it is the essential way in which they are, because they must demand and receive is nothing less than their very being. They receive their life from those who made them gods. And this life, these gods are ready to receive it, quite concretely, from those who bestowed it upon them. This is what is expressed in the idea of sacrifice. Quite literally, a sacrifice "makes-sacred." To these gods, one must sacrifice something; there is always something for which one must die. That for which one can die, in order to give it life, is a god.

27 Voltaire, *Zadig*; G. Flaubert, *La Tentation de saint Antoine*; etc.
28 Aristophanes, *Assembly of Women*, vv. 779–83.

One will notice that this is very close to the definition of what we today call a "value." A famous verse of Juvenal spoke of "losing the reasons for life in order to save one's life" (*Propter vitam vivendi perdere causas*).[29] One can make the obvious retort: one can also lose one's life because of the reasons for life. Here, though, one has to acknowledge a certain legitimacy to Nietzsche's critique: to seek for the meaning of life outside of life is to judge it vis-à-vis something else, and thus to devalue it, to deprive it of its value, even when one thought he was conferring it.[30]

Without the true God who *only* gives life, the final god cannot be anything other than what, in the final analysis, receives all of life, that is, death. After "the death of God" proclaimed by Nietzsche's Zarathustra, the final god is therefore death. Europe began to be aware of this in the nineteenth century, first of all among the most lucid of its writers. This was the case with C. F. Meyer, in a long novella written in the same year as *Zarathustra*. Its hero, who alone knows that the wound from which he suffers is mortal, speaks of death as "his divinity."[31] The Swiss Catholic theologian Hans Urs von Balthasar (1905–88), in his first book, *Apokalypse der deutschen Seele* (*the Apocalypse of the German Soul*), entitled the third volume, published in 1939, "the divinization of death."[32] Everything occurs as if we were in the process of rendering a greater and greater worship to this final god: the fact

29 Juvenal, *Saturae*, VIII, 84.
30 F. Nietzsche, *Fragment de l'automne 1887*, 10 [192], KSA, t. 12, p. 571.
31 C. F. Meyer, *Die Versuchung des Pescara. Novelle* (Stuttgart, Reclam, 1972 [1886]), chap. 3, p. 72; chap. 4, pp, 83, 106; chap. 5, pp. 109–11. This work was brought to my attention by H. Meier, "Der Tod als Gott. Eine Anmerkung zu Martin Heidegger," in *Das theologisch-politische Problem. Zum Thema von Leo Strauss*, Stuttgart, Metzler, 2003, pp. 71–82, especially pp. 79–80.
32 H. U. v. Balthasar, *Apokalypse der deutschen Seele*, v. 3: *Die Vergöttlichung des Todes* (Salzbourg, A. Pustet, 1939. Reed: Einsiedeln, Johannes Verlag, 1998.)

that it was named only indirectly and by euphemism is not the least of the signs of this. Our "civilization" more and more clearly organized itself around this implicit worship. To be sure, this is often done in an involuntary or unacknowledged way. But sometimes it lets itself be seen across certain images, especially certain practices of automutilation; in them we see a fascination with death and its somber godhead.

One cannot die *for* the true God, who has nothing to do with our sacrifice. In contrast, one eventually can die *with* him, if he has arranged it to share our condition. In contrast to the "pagan" gods who demand sacrifices, Augustine opposes the figure of the "true god" who causes the heavenly city, who gives himself rather than demanding anything at all. The city is itself the sacrifice (*cujus verum sacrificium ipsa sit*).[33] Here, one can correct a rather widespread error concerning what is called "the sacrifice of the intellect," which is often used to caricature the Christian faith. It does not refer to the objective genitive, as though one has to sacrifice one's intellect, "humiliate proud reason," etc. It's what grammarians call a subjective genitive: it is the intellect that offers sacrifice. The classical formulation is a transparent allusion to the idea of "rational worship" (*logikè latreia*) express in *Romans*, 12, 1, that is, of a relationship to God that does not involve material sacrificial victims, but which is located, and entirely involves, the reason and liberty of man who thus enters into contact with God.

Let us once again cite the famous formula of St. Irenaeus of Lyon: "The glory of God is the living man."[34] One must understand by this: God does not work for himself. Creation is not an investment from which he awaits, or expects, a return. What glorifies God is nothing other than the very life he gives to his creation, among others, to man. This life, continues Irenaeus, is

---

33 St. Augustine, *The City of God*, XVIII, liv, 2, PL, 41, 620 [d], BA, t. 36, p. 688.

34 St. Irenaeus, *Contre les hérésies*, IV, 20, 7, ed. A. Rousseau (*Sources chrétiennes*, n. 100, Paris, Le Cerf, 1965), p. 647.

"the vision of God." The purpose of God in letting himself be seen is nothing other than to give life.

Conclusion: The "meaning of life"

A bit too often people speak of "the meaning of life." This phrase itself only goes back about a century.[35] Sometimes it is used for apologetic purposes and one therefore means: "Faith gives meaning to life. It would be impossible to live if life didn't have meaning. Hence, we need faith." There can be some truth in that. But Christianity does not propose to give meaning to life, as if life did not have meaning and there was need to seek for some outside of it. Christianity, rather, proposes to *unveil* this meaning.

Life cannot have meaning except as *resurrection*: this is what several acute minds felt in the nineteenth century, and later.[36] Nietzsche sought the affirmation of life in the eternal return of the same. It seems that he elaborated this idea in order to replace the idea of the resurrection of the body that St. Paul had conceived – or rather, the understanding Nietzsche had of St. Paul.[37] On the broad point, Nietzsche was right. The disagreement between him and Christianity bears upon the nature of eternal life, of the meaning of its eternity. The meaning of life is nothing other than life itself, but eternal life.

God does not ask or demand anything of us. He awaits us to accept what he gives us, that we would let him operate in us the gift of this eternal life.

---

35 See J. Grondin, *Du sens de la vie. Essai philosophique* (Quebec, Bellarmin, 2003), pp. 17–25.
36 See, for example, E. Renan, *Dialogues philosohiques*, 3. Rêves [1876], in *Oeuvres Complètes* (Paris, Calmann-Levy, 1947), t. 1, p. 626; and T. W. Adorno, *Negative Dialektik* (Francfort, Suhrkamp, 1966), pp. 207 & 393.
37 D. Franck, *Nietzsche et l'ombre de Dieu* (Paris, PUF, 1998).

Chapter 7
A God Who Forgives Sins

The God who speaks is also the one who recalls what is good and what is bad, who recommends doing good and avoiding evil. He is the one who expects us to choose the good, and with it, life. The living and life-giving God is he who delivers life from what falsifies and wounds it. What injures human life, Christianity calls "sin." The Christian God is one who pardons sins. This is why the Creed confesses "the remission of sins." This is a phrase that we should clarify.

I. Some clarifications

Here at the outset one encounters some lexical difficulties. They bear upon each of the two terms of the phrase.

In our days, the first term, "remission," lends itself to confusion. In contemporary parlance, the verb "remit" is used almost exclusively in juridical, or medical, contexts. One remits a penalty, one speaks of the remission of a disease, cancer, for example. In the latter case, it isn't exactly a cure, but it is the temporary cessation of the disease, which we also say "is unforgiving." Now, to speak of "the remission of sins," to say "your sins are forgiven," is to speak of pardon, and in the fullest since of the term. We will even see that this term ("pardon") is itself inadequate to fully account for the meaning of remission.

On the other hand, the term "sin" is even harder to use today without risking misunderstandings. For the majority of people today it contains a number of vague, even disturbing, connotations. And as for the contemporary understanding of what the Church teaches on this subject – it is often the opposite of the truth. All this is so true that I believe one has to start by taking on these misconceptions. They bar the way to understanding what sin is, the sin that Christians confess that God forgives.

1. Sin and pleasure

First of all, one has to sever the rather foolish association often made which identifies sin with pleasure (whether one does this in a negative or a positive manner). An advertisement used to declare: "It's such a pleasure that it is almost a sin." If I remember correctly, it was a matter of something to eat. The sin in question was gluttony, the "cute sin" (*péché mignon*) or "weakness" that has given many a bakery or candy store its name. Most of the time, however, those who identify sin and pleasure reduce it to the sexual domain. This is a reduction about which the historians have a good deal to tell us, and which began pretty much in modern times. That "making love" causes pleasures, everyone agrees. . . . But the reduction of sin to pleasure, and to sexual pleasure, is a datable phenomenon. It does not come from Christianity which in matters of sexual morality only reprised the philosophical or medical commonplaces of classical antiquity.[1] Nor is it medieval: Dante, for example, places sins of the flesh at the very beginning of Hell, as the least grave of all.[2]

The aforementioned reduction coincided with the rationalization of the Western spirit, tied to a capitalist economy and to the Enlightenment. It was a matter of encouraging the seriousness of work, of thrift, and of not putting one's health at risk.[3] The fact that the reduction of sin to sexuality tends to become more the

1 Even if his historical knowledge is often second-hand, Michel Foucault still has the merit of having recalled this fact; see M. Foucault, *Histoire de la sexualité*, 2. *L'usage des plaisirs* (Paris, Gallimard, 1984), pp. 20–1 ff.
2 Dante, *Divina Commedia*, Inferno, canto V.
3 For example, the physicians of the Enlightenment were much more obsessed with the dangers of masturbation than were the confessors of the Counter-Reformation.

norm as the years pass is, to my mind, one of the signs of the frightening lack of imagination that characterizes modern man: not to find sin anything more interesting than sexual excess seems to me to be a serious flattening of the spirit. There are men who imagine that the "last temptation of Christ," hence the supreme, most important, temptation, had to be – not power or pride – but to sleep with Mary Madalene. In this way, they show where their treasure, that is, their hearts are, manifesting not so much a lack of virtue as a lack of ambition.

In reality, sin does not at all coincide with pleasure: vis-à-vis pleasure, it is indifferent. Let us limit ourselves to recalling this truism: every sin is not a source of pleasure. In saying this, I do not want to make the claim (which is, however, true) that sin deprives us of more substantial joys for the sake of lesser and passing ones, that it constitutes a kind of defective calculation. This is what the English utilitarians endlessly repeated, thereby presenting "sin" almost exclusively as intemperance, above all in matters of alcohol. What I mean to say is that there are sins whose very exercise is a displeasure.

The best example is the sin of envy. It is a distinct, even independent, sin, taking its place among the seven Cardinal sins enumerated by the classical spiritual tradition. Now, this sin is characterized by the fact that it brings no pleasure, it is even defined as the sadness or pain of the soul before another's good.[4] "It is a terrible sentiment. Envy is of all sins the worst because it provides no intrinsic pleasure, in this different from luxury, gluttony, sloth, and even pride. It is hardly human. Men sin in seeking their good and they find it, at least partly, in sinning, but envy installs the person in pure evil, disinterested evil we might say, an angelic (or demonic) evil, without pleasure. It comes upon men suddenly and possesses them. This is why the duty to avoid it figures in the tenth, and final, place of the list of commandments."[5]

---

4   To cite only pagan authors: Xenophon, *Memorabilia*, III, 9, 8; Plato, *Philebus*, 47e, 48b, 50a; Aristotle, *Rhetoric*, II, 10, 1387b23.
5   A. Besançon, *Une génération* (Paris, Julliard, 1987), p. 267.

Next, I would like to recall that there is even a sin whose pain and punishment does not merely accompany the act but constitutes it. Today, this sin is somewhat forgotten, even if it continues to be practiced today as much as in the past. Nonetheless, it did not fail to be listed in the traditional enumeration of Cardinal sins, and it has its own titles of nobility in world literature, in Dante and Petrarch, for example. It is the sin that consists in willingly despairing and resigning oneself to sadness (*tristitia spiritualis boni*) – what the spiritual tradition called "acedia."[6]

Finally, I would like to recall that sin not only does not have a necessary connection with pleasure but, on the contrary, it can be the cause of a diminution of pleasure. This, at least, is what St. Thomas teaches. According to him, the first sin, that of Adam in the Garden of Eden, led to a loss of sexual pleasure. If Adam had not sinned, this pleasure would have been even more intense, because better integrated in the rational project of life and more subject to liberty.[7]

2. Offending God?

The false idea according to which sin would, essentially, be a source of pleasure is compounded by the perversion of an otherwise correct formulation – one, however, that is often misunderstood – according to which sin "offends God." "My God, I am heartily sorry for having offended you." Catholics used to say in the act of contrition they recited when receiving absolution, after having confessed. What did they understand by that? That God is offended does not, of course, mean that he suffered any sort of diminishment or detriment. Sin does not inflict some wound on God for which one must compensate. It does not wound his body, because he does not have one. Nor does it wound his honor, which would require recompense. The one who is harmed by sin is not

6 See my article, "L'image et l'acédie. Remarques sur le premier Apophtegme," *Revue thomiste*, 85, 1985, pp. 201–6.
7 St. Thomas, *Commentary on the Sentences*, II, distinction 20, q. 1, art. 2, ad 2; *Summa theologiae*, I, q. 98, art. 2, ad 3.

the one "against whom" one appears to sin but the one who commits it. An Old Testament prophet already put on God's lips this question: "Is it me that they wound (*le-hakh'is*)? . . . Is it not rather themselves, to their own confusion (*le-ma'an boshet peney-hem*)? (*Jeremiah*, 7, 9). In sinning, it is the sinner who abases him-self. God is not "offended" but by what abases man who is his creature. Here one must cite St. Thomas, who brings everything together in a magnificent formulation: "God is not offended by us except in the measure that we act against our own good."[8]

The erroneous conceptions of "the offense" that sin would inflict on God come from a widespread idea according to which we find ourselves in a relation of rivalry with God, where what one party has, the other is deprived of. This presupposes that God and man dispute the possession of certain goods that are suscepti-ble of interesting both, and whose limited quantity would make it that their appropriation would deprive one party. This is a rather naïve hydrostatic: if the level rises at one end, it dips at the other.[9] This naiveté, however, is at the root of a purported modern "Prometheanism" which, in its theoretical aspect (e.g., Feuerbach's critique of religion) and in its practical aspect, aims to recoup for man what he initially would have yielded by projecting it upon God. From this point of view, one can do more than invoke "the sweetness of sin." Such a purportedly radical attitude could admit the obvious, that sin is not always pleasant, but do so as an *apologia* for a kind of heroism. Sin – whether it be pleasant or not – would be a blow against the celestial tyrant.

In truth, though, the choice is not between God and us, but between, on one hand, a false image of God and us, and, on the other, the reality of the relation which connects us to God, that is, the reality that God is the object of our fulfillment, of our good. The human being who sins only wounds himself, by depriving himself of his good. To sin is not to appropriate a good that would

8 St. Thomas, *Summa contra Gentiles*, III, 122, ad initium.
9 This image is found in Nietzsche, *Die Fröhliche Wissenscha*ft, IV, #285, KSA, v. 3, p. 528.

belong to God. In the final analysis, whether man wrongly arrogates to himself what does not belong to him, or whether he wrests back what God would have usurped, makes hardly any difference. Both these ways of seeing things rest on the same error, in that they both imagine that the Good is what God possesses. The Good, however, is not what God has: the Good is what God is. God is the Good of man. To sin, to separate oneself from God, and to injure oneself: these make one.

That is why sin is essentially damage, in the sense of injury. And also in the sense of "too bad!" when confronting something defective or ruined. In some places, popular discourse still speaks of sin this way. One hears, for example: "It would be a sin to waste that food without finishing it." In Italian, the most usual way of expressing what we mean when we say "Too bad!" is, precisely, *peccato*! Gianni Vattimo has briefly meditated upon this manner of speaking, in a way that seems to me to touch upon something essential.[10]

3. Sin presupposes forgiveness

A mistake that, perhaps, is even more freighted with consequences for our understanding is the one that consists in separating the two terms, "remission" and "sin," which are united in the Christian confession of faith. Once they are separated, the two ideas are placed in a certain order, according to which the idea of sin occupies the first place. A certain Christian apologetics has succumbed to this temptation. It proceeds by attempting to convince man (and above all, "modern man," who is deemed to be more difficult to convince. . .) that he is a sinner and that he therefore has need of redemption (which, then, would be proposed to him, in second place).[11] In this optic, one can lament the purported "loss of the sense of sin," as if it complicated the matter, even made it impossible, because depriving forgiveness of its foundation.

---

10 See G. Vattimo, *Espérer croire, op. cit.*, pp. 97–105.

11 Here one can recognize the criticisms of D. Bonhoeffer which are rather close to those of Nietzsche, letter of June 8, 1944, in *Widerstand und Ergebung*, Gütersloh, GTB Siebenstern, p. 159–160.

In so doing, one allows oneself to be misled by an analogy. Most often, of course, the evil precedes the remedy, and it is necessary to become aware of the evil in order to experience the need for the remedy. Thus, because I see that my teeth are crooked, I know that I need to go to the dentist. However, the Creed confesses faith in "the remission of sins," not in sin. What is an article of faith is *not* sin, but rather its remission. It is therefore imperative to comprehend that implications of this inversion, especially since it is so paradoxical vis-à-vis our ordinary experience of good and evil.

As for our ordinary experience, it presents several facets, which it is useful to distinguish, if only quickly.

a) On one hand, evil presents itself as the fact that something "goes badly," "has something wrong." If you want to speak pedantically, one would say: it is "dysfunctional." What ought to work without a problem but which is disturbed is, precisely, the well-working of a system. This system can be a mechanism (broken) or an organism (illness), or even a society ("social breakdown"). The evil is done away with by some repair that should make all these up-and-running.

In such cases, pardon has no place, because of the lack of an object to which it could be given. Forgiveness can only be bestowed on a person who has done something wrong. Here, however, there is no one one can forgive. How can one forgive a motor-part, a diseased organ, a "society"? Even more so, how can one forgive nature for an earthquake or devastating flood? We recognize the need for a person, a guilty party, when we try at all costs to find someone to blame. A social upheaval has to be the work of some conspirators. And after a natural catastrophe, we demand the person or agency that ought to have foreseen it, that ought to have warned us against it, that should have been better prepared. Someone to forgive thus appears as a kind of photographic negative, in the form of a scape-goat.

b) Evil also presents itself as the violation of a civil law. The transgression is repaired by the punishment of the guilty party. Here one can see intimations of forgiveness: amnesty or pardon. Still, one needs to ask if these anticipations do not obey a logic different from that of positive law. Perhaps they are the fruit of a rather calculating prudence or of political calculation, an attempt to render public opinion well-disposed on the eve of an election. As for the pardoning privilege of the executive, one can see in it the outdated relic of the divine origin of the royalty, and hence, something no longer to be tolerated.[12] In the two cases, whether one goes beyond strict justice from low motives or high, one does not come to something similar to pardon except by leaving the domain proper to law.

c) Evil can be a misdeed committed against the moral law, which one fails to observe. The moral law as such cannot sanction the one who violates it; it cannot pardon him either. It is only a norm by which one can measure the conduct of men, which remains indifferent to the attitude they take vis-à-vis it. It makes sin known (*Romans*, 3, 20), but without the power to avoid it. It is not the speed limit sign that goes on to accuse the motorist who drives too fast. Here, what makes pardon impossible is not, as in the first case, the absence of an object who can be pardoned; it is, rather, the absence of a subject capable of pardoning.

d) Finally, evil can be a wrong against a person. It is overcome when the one who commits it makes reparation. The reparation itself does not vary, whether the wrong falls under the law or not. Whether I restore an object willingly or under constraint, the act of restoration is the same. On the other hand, one also sees the possibility emerge of entering into the domain of the personal as such, and not merely that of juridical obligation. I can ask the one I have injured for forgiveness, and he can (or can not) grant it to me.

It is at this point that the analogy with the remission of sins is at once the closest and the most misleading. In an initial approximation, one can very well say that God "forgives" our sins. But

---

12 See K. Marx, *Kritik der hegelschen Rechtsphilosophie*, #282, in Werke (Berlin, Dietz), t. 1, p. 237.

forgiveness is not yet remission. Forgiveness is something human. The remission of sins can only come from God. In truth, when someone forgives a wrong I have committed against him, he thus ceases to consider me as a wrong-doer and as definitively marked by my misdeed. But he can do no more. To be sure, he can turn his eyes away from what I did and attempt to forget it, and to look only to the future. But he cannot change me, he cannot change my heart. He cannot restore my liberty of not-sinning. God alone is capable of that, and this is what he does by remitting my sins. Remission is a liberation.

II. My sin

1. Where is evil?

The remission that God alone is capable of granting transcends human forgiveness. Similarly, sin transcends all other forms of evil, including the type with which it is often mistaken, what I earlier called "misdeed." Sin is distinguished from other forms of evil by its location, by the distinctive way one must answer the question, "Where is sin?" To the question, several answers can, and in fact have, been given. Evil can be placed in certain regions of the physical world. In ancient cosmology it was the domain of the sublunar, of matter deemed to be impure, in contingency.[13] One can make it the cause of the illusion of man, who believes that he is the end and purpose of the universe, which in itself is above – it is isn't beyond – good and evil. One can situate it in the biological past of *homo sapiens*, who has transmitted to his descendents the trait called "aggressivity." Finally, it can be located in the ill-workings of institutions created by man. However, speaking precisely, one can call none of these phenomena "sin." At most, they are defects, perverse effects, and the like. Where then is sin?

In me. In me only. Chesterton was asked by a newspaper to answer the question, What is wrong in the world? He responded

13 See my work, *The Wisdom of the World*, p. 108–111.

with a great laconic answer: "Dear sirs, I am. Sincerely yours." He had a thousand reasons for this answer. I alone can accuse myself of sin. I can observe that someone else commits a misdeed. But I do not have the right to accuse anyone else of sin. This in fact would itself be a sin. Of myself alone can I say that I am fully responsible for what I did. In contrast, I can always say about the other person, that if I had been in his place, I would, perhaps, have sinned even more greviously. I can disapprove of his conduct, I even have to do so if it violates the moral law. But do I have the right to judge him to be a sinner, worthy of receiving the wage of sin which is death (*Romans*, 7, 23)? I certainly have no right to say of anyone else that he is wholly a sinner, and thus to assign him to the place where sin is alone with itself, eternally confronting itself, and where persons (if there are any there) only stand with their backs to one another. One of the Desert Fathers of Egypt has a damned person say: "It is impossible to see anyone face-to-face; we are found only with our backs to each other."[14] I do not have the right to send anyone to hell, even the worst criminals known to history. Why? Among other reasons, because I always have to ask myself: what would I have done in his place, with his character, his past, and the particular circumstances in which he found himself?

To be sure, most of us have never committed a crime, must less organized genocide. But this is not really the question. If the gravity of a misdeed is measured by the extent to which it affects another, it is obvious that it is graver to eliminate a nation than to wear the tie of a college one did not attend. But this is not the way to sound the depths of the way in which a fault affects me personally. This has to be measured in the light of the possibility (or not) I had to commit the fault. We have never massacred Hutus. But we are not Tusis. It is not difficult to avoid what we had no chance of doing; nothing is easier than congratulating oneself about resisting temptations one's never experienced. A pagan philosopher, Epictetus, already made the point. One of his students committed an error of logic and, seeing the vehemence

14 *Apophtegmes des Pères du désert*, Abba Macaire, 38.

with which his teacher reproved him, said that this was less serious than killing one's father. Epictetus replied in so many words: "Did you ever have the opportunity to kill him? You had an opportunity not to make a mistake in your academic lesson, and you failed to do so. Something tells me that if you had the chance to kill your father, you would take it."[15]

Hell only exists in the first person singular. We, therefore, need to rework a famous phrase (Sartre's "Hell is the other people."). We should say, Hell is everyone, except for everyone else. In other words, me alone. If, however, sin only exists in the first person singular, it is not in sin that the person becomes a person! O quite the contrary, sin is depersonalization, the worst depersonalization. But it is a depersonalization that comes from the person, it is a sort of suicide, one that touches the person in his very core. It is not surprising, therefore, that, conversely, the one called "the devil" is the personification of the impersonal as such.[16]

2. "For every sin, mercy"

But if this is the case, everything must be turned around. The proverb "For every sin, mercy" is well-known. It seems to me, however, that it contains unsuspected depths, like the statements Hegel called "speculative propositions." In them, the predicate that is initially ascribed to the subject takes precedent and becomes the subject itself. Sin is rightly defined as that for which there is mercy, and nothing else. In fact, it is dangerous to speak of sin without forgiveness, even to speak of it before speaking of forgiveness. To do so is to confuse it with fault. One can very well speak of fault without speaking of forgiveness. Fault in fact is defined vis-à-vis an instance that cannot pardon, because it isn't a

---

15 Epictetus, *Entretiens*, I, 7, 30–32, ed. H. Schenkl (Leipzig, Teubner, 1894), p. 29.

16 I bring together in this last sentence the insights of Jean-Luc Marion, "Le mal en personne," in *Prolégomènes à la charité* (Paris, La Difference, 1986), pp. 13–42. For formulations similar to mine, see pp. 37 & 41–42.

person: a law that one has transgressed, an idea (usually vain) of oneself that one has belied. In contrast, the only way to define sin is to say: sin is what is forgiven. One can even say: it has no other meaning than to be forgiven.

If a fault is quite visible, if one can see its evidence in a deed, sin is only visible from the perspective of forgiveness. It is therefore only so after the fact, in retrospect, looking over one's shoulder, perhaps because it has no face to see initially. Sin is like a precipice toward which one returns after having just risked falling in. If he had fallen in, he could not have seen its depth, not having survived the fall. This is why Pascal has Christ address these words to a penitent: "To the extent that you expiate [your sins] you will know them and it will be said to you: go, your sins are forgiven."[17]

God alone can forgive sin, because sin is evil appropriated, personalized, translated into the first person. Here, one can risk a hardy phrase and assert the paradox that in a certain way only God knows persons. In so doing, one diametrically opposes the famous thesis of certain medieval Aristotelians, according to which God only knows genera, hence his providence can only be exercised on them, not on individuals.[18] In this way, God watches out for the preservation of the human race in general, but not on particular individuals.

Here one can defend the contrary thesis, one that was magnificently expressed by an author one rarely thinks of in this connection: Tocqueville

> God does not at all think of the human race in general. He sees at once, and individually, all the beings of which humanity is composed, and he perceive each of them with the resemblances that liken him to all and the differences that distinguish him. God has no need of general ideas; he has never felt the need of containing a great number of

17 Pascal, "Le mystère de Jesus," #553, op. cit., t. 2, p. 439.
18 See, for example, Al-Ghazâlî, *The Incoherence of the Philosophers* [*Tahâfut al-Falâsifa*], 11th discussion, ed. M. E. Marmura (Brigham Young University Press, 1997), p. 128–33.

analogous objects under the same form in order to be able to think.[19]

If this is the case, only God can forgive sin once it is assumed by a person. He cannot forgive defects, or wrongs, or hereditary traits, if they remain in their impersonal form. He cannot do so, any more than we ourselves can.

One therefore should not ask if God *can* forgive all sins, as if his generosity is limited. One, rather, should reverse the question, put it in the passive, and ask if sin *can be forgiven* by God. This would entail asking: on what condition is evil capable of being forgiven? It can be so, only if God knows it, if God knows *what evil* to forgive. Now, in theology an entire tradition of thought influenced by neoplatonism maintains that God does not know, and cannot know, evil as such, because evil as such does not exist, it is only the negation of good.[20] What exists is good perverted or corrupted. Kiekegaard, for example, puts himself in this tradition what he writes: "On can say . . . of God that he has no knowledge of evil. . . . The fact that God does not know evil, that he does not and cannot know it, this is the absolute punishment of evil."[21]

Forgiveness cannot attain evil except when evil, which is the non-personal par excellence, even the anti-personal, takes on a personal aspect. And it is me, me alone, who can give one to it by recognizing it as my own. This is why sin is not forgiven unless it is acknowledged. This is the case for Catholics in the sacrament formerly called "penitence" or "confession," and which these days is called "reconciliation." In a sense this acknowledgment is the condition of forgiveness, but it the paradoxical sense of the word we developed earlier. We are not forgiven on the condition

19 A. de Tocqueville, *De la démocratie en Amérique*, II, 1, 3, in *Oeuvres*, t. II, ed. A. Jardin (Paris, Gallimard, 1992), p. 523.

20 See J.-M. Garrigues, *Dieu sans idée du mal. La liberté de l'homme au coeur de Dieu* (Paris, Critérion, 1982).

21 S. Kierkegaard, *The Concept of Anxiety*, Chap. IV, trad. P.-H. Tisseau, in *Oeuvres Complètes*, t. VII (Paris, Éditions de l'Orante, 1973), pp. 208–9.

of acknowledgment, as a sort of recompense for whatever this avowal, whether expressed in the confessional or in the internal forum, contains that is painful. What this avowal permits is not forgiveness, which is given from eternity, but rather the possibility of taking hold of it (if I can put it that way) and of being liberated by it. This is why it would be better to translate the Latin formula which concludes sacramental confession, *ego te absolvo*, not as: "I pardon you," but rather, more literally, by: "I unbind you, I loosen your bonds."

If accepting the personal appropriation of sin produces forgiveness, not to do so excludes one from forgiveness. This is not because I then would commit one more sin (which is, however, true). It is because I do not "give" to evil what makes it available for forgiveness. I leave it in the impersonal condition in which I myself am plunged, thereby rendering it as it were invisible to God.

Once, however, sin is recognized by the one who confesses it, it enters into contact with its contrary. "I have sinned" is, on one hand, the sole true sentence concerning sin, since sin can only be committed by an "I," it can only exist in the first person singular. But at the same time it is a contradictory formula, because sin cannot coexist with the person as such and it dissolves at the person's contact. In this way, sin is the contrary of what is often said about it. In it, one typically sees an accusation, an affirmation of culpability. But it is when culpability remains vague and diffuse that it is the most hopeless. Who can heal "structures"? Who can overcome an "aggressivity" with roots in the farthest history of humanity? Who can act as if history had not happened? The endeavors to overcome "evil" conceived in this impersonal way, by revolutions, purges, and reeducations, have led to monstrosities.

3. Remission

Once put in contact with the "I," sin disappears. Here, it is not a matter of releasing from his sin an "I" that would have become tarnished, of denying the bad predicates that characterized the subject. This is what the Gnostics taught, with their image of a pure pearl fallen into the dung of this world. Rather, it is a matter of putting back into circulation a subject whose very presence contradicts these predicates, in other words, the personal subject. This is why God does not discharge sin except by restoring the subject to himself and to his liberty. This is exactly what is to be understood by "remission of sins."

The difficulty addressed here is unique, but capital. In order for our sins to be forgiven, it suffices to become (again) a subject. But this is precisely what we cannot do, because sin has paralyzed our personality. We can no more restore our personality than Baron Münchhausen can pull himself up by his braids. We can do nothing in the domain, unless God had not already pardoned us from all eternity in Christ (*Ephesians*, 1, 4).

In this way, to speak of "the remission of sins" is almost a tautology. Sin serves being-pardoned. The witticism of Heinrich Heine on his death-bed is well known (even if it we cannot know in what spirit it was uttered). He was asked how he was with God. He responded with a smile: "Don't worry! God will forgive me, it's his métier."[22] In a profound sense this is perfectly true. God alone can forgive. If one can put it this way: only He knows how to do this. The saying becomes false, however, when Heine spoke of the future. It would be better to speak of the past. God is not going to forgive us in the future, provided that we are wise. He has forgiven us, once for all time, on the Cross.

God forgives our sins, not in order to recuperate what we would have caused him to lose, but to allow us to recover our lost integrity. Nor does he grant us this remission "on condition," for example, requiring us first of all to love him. "What? A God who loves men, on the condition that they believe in him. . . ." As we saw, this sentiment comes from Nietzsche. This is an absurd demand, for the simple reason that sin is precisely what deprives us of the ability to love, and hence, to believe; the forgiveness of

22 Related in Alfred Meissner, *Heinrich Heine. Erinnerungen*, Hambourg, Hoffmann & Campe, 1856 [=Leipzig, Zentralantiquariat der DDR, 1972], V^e partie: 1854, ch. 5, p. 259.

sin must first of all give us this capacity. Thus, it is by her regained capacity to love that Jesus recognized that the sins of the woman who anointed his feet with oil were forgiven (*Luke*, 7, 47). She had already opened herself, even if obscurely, to the hope of her being reintegrated into the plan of salvation God had for her.

God does not demand that we love him in return, as if, once it is assumed that we know how to love, we have to choose among different objects, all equally worthy of our love. (An even moderately sincere examination of oneself suffices to establish that, on the contrary, we do not even fulfill the first condition.) And as if God demanded a recompense for services rendered. In reality, he invites us, quite simply, to love; or rather: he allows us to do so. And the love that he frees in us spontaneously orients itself in the direction where it can assume all its amplitude and live according to its proper logic. This "direction" is, precisely, God. God is less the object of love than the space within which I can encounter what (or better: who) to love, to wit: my neighbor. "To love one's neighbor out of the love of God" does not mean: to love one's neighbor by seeking another object of love through him, which would be God. It is better understand as loving one's neighbor because God loves him and makes me capable of loving him.

Conclusion

The fact that remission is in the past is in one way reassuring, since it is something already acquired (at what a price, however!). But in another sense, it has something truly frightening. For it still remains to know whether I accept this forgiveness, if I accept to receive what is always offered us. It belongs to each one of us, therefore, to ask himself: do I truly desire the Good? Am I sure that it is truly God I seek? Do I believe that once I find myself face-to-face with him, I would find myself much more alive and worth attending to?

Index

Abraham, 1, 9–14, 23, 52–53, 86–87, 110, 128
access, 26, 33, 40, 43, 130
acedia, 142
action, 28
Adam, 10, 13, 109, 126–128, 142
adhesion, 41, 134
Adorno, T. W., 138n.
el-Afghanî, Jamâl ed-Din, 14n.
aggressivity, 147, 152
Ahmad Khan, 14n.
Akiba, Rabbi, 72
Ali, 107
Amenophis IV (Akhnaton), 4, 52–53
Amos, 119
analogy, 5, 39, 41, 51, 68–69, 75, 78, 144
angel, 9, 32–33, 126, 141
arianism, 50–51
Aristophanes, 34, 59, 70, 135
Aristotle, 3, 5, 28, 34, 36, 53, 56, 59, 64, 101, 105–106, 118, 132n., 133n., 141n.
Arnaldez, R., 1n.
asking, 124
Assmann, J. 48, 105n.
associating, 8–9, 44, 46, 52, 72
Athanasius, saint, 51
Auerbach, E., 84n.
Augustine, saint, 30, 34n., 41n., 59n., 64, 123n., 133–135, 137
Authority, 78, 80, 110, 113–114, 134
Autonomy, 48, 52, 120
avowal, 152

ba'al, 72

Baeck, L., 2
Baha'is, 4, 16
Balmary, M., 134n.
Balthasar, H. U. von, 82n., 136
Baruzi, J., 82n.
Baudelaire, C., 46n.
Bayer, C., 53n.
belief, 36–38, 96
Bergson, H., 30
Bernanos, G., 103
Bernard of Clairvaux, saint, 58–59
Besançon, A., 141
al-Biruni, 87
Boethius, 32
Bonaventure, saint, 129
Bonhoeffer, D., 144n.
Book, people of the, 15
Bouyer, L., 74n.
Brague, R., 3n., 14n., 93n., 106n., 118n., 142n., 147n.
Buber, M., 81
Buddhism, 3

Cabanis, 34
Candid the Arian, 54
Cathars, 49
Céline, L. F., 129
Celsus, 50
Chanson de Roland, 9n.
charity, 40, 58–59, 64–68, 110
Chateaubriand, F. R. de, 47n.
Chesterton, G. K., 192, 206, 231
christianist, 93
Colpe, C., 87n.
condition, 130, 151–153
conscience, 120
Council of Lateran, IV 55, 58

Index